Abandoning Temples

Jeff Johnson

Published by Jeff Johnson, 2024.

While every precaution has been taken in the preparation of this book, the publisher assumes no responsibility for errors or omissions, or for damages resulting from the use of the information contained herein.

ABANDONING TEMPLES

First edition. November 10, 2024.

Copyright © 2024 Jeff Johnson.

ISBN: 979-8227775467

Written by Jeff Johnson.

Table of Contents

To those with one foot out the door,

those who feel like giving up on God, and

those who feel like God or God's people have given up on them

Introduction

P eace or sword? Which is it?

There's a gospel reading that I've never much cared for:

Jesus said to his Apostles: "Do not think that I have come to bring peace upon the earth. I have come to bring not peace but the sword." He continues: "Whoever loves father or mother more than me is not worthy of me, and whoever loves son or daughter more than me is not worthy of me; and whoever does not take up his cross and follow after me is not worthy of me." (Matthew 10:34-38)

That's not an easy message to take in, though it seems like it captures the mood of this combustible moment.

I think that's because we have an idolatry problem.

We meaning me. We meaning America. We meaning everybody, I suspect.

When I say "idolatry," I don't mean old-school statues to Ba'al or golden calves. I mean anything that we put into the "Whoever loves (fill in the blank) more than me" formula that makes us wince or hesitate. Anything that, if we're honest with ourselves, we can't say we love God more than.

I have a bunch of things that reveal me to be an idolator when I put them into this formula. Do I love my wife and daughter more than God? Yeah, for sure. How about my own pride, ego, and control? Yeah, I love those more than God too.

What about our political party? Our sports team? Our country? Do we love these more than God? It already seems like we in America have chosen our partisan stripes over our brothers and sisters in ways more fundamental than typical sibling rivalry.

We are also idolators when we add other stuff onto the "me" in the "Whoever loves ... more than me." What about our Church? We talk a lot about different brands of belief: Catholic and evangelical and Protestant, traditional and conservative and progressive and patriotic, even. Do we love our brand of *following* God more than we love God Himself? It seems like we would rather have a version of god that likes our politics and our country (and our football team), and hates the other guys, even if that's not the one that shows up in the Bible talking about loving your enemy and caring for the left out.

The "peace or sword" thing is especially challenging when you look at other parts of the Bible, like the Mass readings for the sixteenth Sunday of ordinary time (which is July 21 in 2024). If that first passage's Jesus is all about the sword and division, look at these readings. Jeremiah says "Woe to the shepherds who mislead and scatter the flock of my pasture, says the Lord." Jeremiah goes on to say that God "will appoint shepherds for them who will shepherd them so that they need no longer fear and tremble; and none shall be missing, says the Lord." The Psalm on that Sunday is Psalm 23, "The Lord is my shepherd," all about peace that fears no evil. "Only goodness and kindness follow me all the days of my life," it says at the end. Then St. Paul in Ephesians 2: "For [Christ] is our peace, he who made both [the far off and near] one and broke down the dividing wall of enmity, ... establishing peace. ... He came and preached peace to you who were far off and peace to those who were near." And the Gospel, Mark 6, has Jesus trying to pull his gang away to rest a while, because they were so inundated by crowds. When He realizes that the crowds have followed Him to his attempted retreat spot, "his heart was moved with pity for them, for they were like sheep without a shepherd."

So which is it? Peace or sword?

The shepherd that Jeremiah says God wants for people is one that conquers fear and trembling and lets nobody go missing. The God that Paul touts breaks down walls of enmity and preaches peace to far and near. The Jesus that Mark finds has a heart moved with pity.

That kind of God wouldn't be universally popular here right now. A bunch of us are all-in on fear, addicted to media that induce trembling as a business model. We want the people who are far from us

- politically, ethnically, religiously - to stay that way; in fact, we might rather they go away altogether, especially if we're convinced that they are intent on destroying everything we love. If someone were to say that your politics were idolatrous, or that your patriotism was crowding out God, or that God deserves more of your energy than your football team, well, that person might lose a couple friends (and maybe a sibling or two). They'd also have a hard time finding a welcoming community of fellow believers. Maybe that's the sword that a Gospel of peace brings today, one we swing for (and at) ourselves.

Personally, I'm pretty tired of the idols; (frankly, I'm just tired, period). I would rather just picnic by a pool in the grass somewhere than watch us continue to gouge out each other's eyes.

It takes a lot of work, I've found, to root out the addictions to fear and accept those who are far and near. It takes practice to grow a heart that can be moved by people I don't agree with, and I still struggle with that. The temples to the gods of pride and control and distraction are harder to quit than a gym membership.

Maybe you think this is unrealistic, pie-in-the-sky stuff. Maybe you think abandoning these temples to perpetually angry gods is complicity with your enemy.

Me, I'm ready for some goodness and kindness to follow me around for a while. The only way I know out of this mess is to choose Love, not Fear, whether it's realistic or not. I'm going to keep trying to abandon those temples to the idols I've subscribed to for too long. You can keep the sword.

· · · ·

It was a weird three weeks that sent me down the path of abandoning temples.

I was sitting in a hotel bar in Washington, D.C., in the company of friends and colleagues who were there for a meeting. I was in town for a different reason, a special mission of sorts. I had been invited to the White House, along with other state leaders, to talk with the Administration about what great things the federal government was doing for us.

I was truly dreading it. I had tried to get out of the invitation, even suggested someone else go in my place, but the guidance was clear that I needed to go.

Then, sitting at the hotel bar, things got weirder. "Hey, Jeff, we're going to need you to go to Mar-a-Lago to help us video the former president. Might be early next week, might be a little later." It turned out to be about three weeks later.

Within a span of three weeks, I visited the White House at the invitation of then-President Joe Biden and Mar-a-Lago to meet former President Donald Trump. And in both cases, I dreaded each moment between the opening suggestion to my arrival on site almost identically.

That cross-partisan dread really unsettled me, especially since part of my job with a non-partisan advocacy organization is to interact with elected officials across party lines. I could have understood being excited about both opportunities; meeting the president or visiting the White House is a great honor. I suspect a lot of people would have been excited by one opportunity while dreading the other, depending on their political allegiance. But here I was, dreading both of them. Why would I do that?

I had met a president before (as well as any number of senators, members of Congress and other political luminaries). I had been to the White House before, too. Those experiences had been exciting at the time, and I have fond memories of them. So why did I dread this time?

I realized quickly that this reaction wasn't about either of these presidents; it was about me. If I imagine substituting any other presidents for these two, the dread for the situations would have remained the same. As I have reflected on those three weeks, the image that recurs is one of revisiting temples whose idols I have abandoned, but whose spaces I have not reclaimed. The dread I felt was one of entering a space of worship for false gods that I had once been guilty of worshipping. Gods of politics and celebrity and tribalism.

That realization made me think about all the other idols I have spent too much of my life on. I have unmasked many of them, though I suspect I still have blind spots to others. In some cases, I have found ways to remove those idols from my life almost entirely, bulldozing those temples and building new, healthy structures in their place. In other cases, I've found new purposes for those old temples. In a few cases, I have been able to rededicate them to the one God I know. And in a lot of cases, like politics, I'm still struggling.

This set of reflections on the idols I've abandoned and the temples they inhabited has been a difficult examination of conscience. I don't normally focus on the past, or on the negative; I've found the best way for me to make progress is to crowd out the bad by filling up life with the better. Nevertheless, I am sharing these in case they connect to something you're going through. I hope it helps us both.

As I entered the process of putting this together, I realized that, in order to truly appreciate the nature of idolatry, it's worth first spending time focusing on the true God that actually *deserves* our worship. There is a simple prayer that St. Francis of Assisi's first followers related hearing Francis repeat over and over: "Who are You, O Lord, and who am I?" (We should all gain some comfort from the fact that one of Christianity's greatest saints got stuck on those questions, too.) For reasons that will probably become clear, I don't think you can answer the first question without also reflecting on the second, and I'm using those questions to string together the first part of the book. I'll close with the reflections on idols.

One final note: These reflections have been written over a period of several years. To give readers additional context, for any reflections written before 2023, I've added the month I initially published the essay on ReadingFrancis.com at the end of the chapter.

Who Are You, O Lord?

Here's the bottom line: God is the one who is not an idol. As atheists are keen to point out, this is the conceit of every religion. *All y'all worship the wrong deity; but ours is totally legit.* Atheists just disbelieve in one god more than believers, after all.

You will not see me try to prove God exists here, because it's no more something I'm interested in than trying to prove that my wife exists, or that I do. Know someone well enough, and the question of their existence evaporates as so much philosophical navel-gazing.

Here, though, are some reflections from over the years on who this God is that I have bumped into and what God is about. Reflections about God's immanence, God's love and mercy, God's compassion and suffering with us. Those are the parts of God I know well enough to be certain of.

Who God is matters a lot. There are a lot of idols — like greed and power and lust — that are pretty easy to point to. Those are batting practice fastballs that many people are eager to take swings at. But if God is more interested in love and mercy than being "respectable" or even following all the rules, then it becomes a lot clearer for Christians that idols aren't all "out *there*," in the big, bad world. They're *right here*, in each of our hearts and at the core of our communities, including the ones we think of as holy.

So let's talk about the "one God more" that I know and the idols that God reveals.

God is Not So Hard to Find

God is not so hard to find.

We tend to think that God is far away from this world. We think this place is just awful, and it's not hard to find evidence to back that view up. If there is a god, we think, it's got to be one who keeps his distance. Maybe He drops some clues around so that if we look hard, we can find him. But on the whole, this is no place for divinity.

Early Christianity wrestled with a viral variant called Gnosticism that pushed the notion that this world was rotten to the core, and that only by escaping to some other spiritual world, like billionaires in a spaceship, could we find holy relief. Gnostics claimed that there were some secret codes you needed to get out of this world, to where God was.

A lot of us are still a little bit Gnostic. If you look around, you can see whatever evil repulses you the most — immorality, injustice, hatred, corruption — it seems like it's in your face everywhere you turn. Gnostic cheat codes sound like a good option if you think you need to get out of here to find rest.

But God is not so hard to find.

Francis of Assisi has a reputation as a nature lover; he's the patron saint of the ecology and there are stories of him talking to birds and wolves (doesn't everyone?) and he was known to relocate worms he found in the road so they wouldn't get hurt and he popularized nativity scenes with live animals and he wrote a whole canticle about creatures. But he wasn't so much a nature lover as he was someone who bought all the way into the weirdness of Christ in a couple of big ways.

We say that Christ is the one "through whom all things were made." When God creates, He speaks things into being, and Christ is the Word that makes it happen (check out Genesis 1: "And God said ... and so there was.") If that's not enough, Christ, fully God, becomes fully human and walks around with us other humans, not only preaching and healing but eating and drinking and noticing flowers and birds and stuff. And then He is really, horribly lynched. And then He proves that lynching won't stop Love.

You know how people will sometimes go nuts over being someplace where a famous person was — growing up, the clichè was signs that said "Elvis slept here;" I think before that it was "George Washington slept here"? It's as if the fact that you can inhabit the same place a famous person once inhabited brings that place extra specialness, even if it's a Motel 6 or a rundown bed and breakfast.

Christ walking around on the Earth meant, for Francis, that every ounce of ground could have a sign that said "God walked here." Everything about this place could have a sign that said "God made this special." Francis saw that everything and everyone was holy, not on their own, but because God cared about them enough to join us here.

In the Peanuts' Christmas special, Pigpen waxes poetic about how the dirt billowing off of him may have been trod on by Nebuchadnezzar; so, for Francis, every piece of dirt was spoken into being by God, was embraced by God-made-flesh, and is still deeply loved by the living God. Therefore we ought to love it the same way, not by running from it like the Gnostics, but by hugging it like it reflects the loving God who made it. If the Word is God and looks like water and seeds and fruit and dirt, then you can find reflections everywhere. God is not so hard to find.

But maybe the dirt just looks like dirt to you. And maybe the ugliness around us blots out the beauty. Even if God is rain and flowers and flocks and harvests, look at the weather and you see blistering heat and wildfires and destructive storms. Or maybe you're expecting God to look like angels and stained glass and halos, and that's not what you see here.

Sometimes I ask people to join me in a sort of *examen*: Where did you see love? Where did you spot joy? Where did you see beauty? Where did you find peace? It's a practice of God-spotting.

We say that God is Love. We say that the fruits of the Spirit also include joy and peace and a whole lot more. When we see those things around us, they are reflections of the God who made them. And even in the ugliness, if you look, you can find them.

God is not so hard to find. God may not look like what we expected. We may not see as much as we'd like. But I promise you this: the more you look for love and joy and peace and beauty, the more you will find.

We put the wrong aspect of God in the center.

I don't get many requests for theological opinions. (Perhaps that's a hint I should have taken a long time ago.) But one of my sisters, of all people, asked me a question, and it's a good one: Does God cause bad things to happen so that we'll be drawn closer to Him?

Of course, the only real answer I can offer is "I don't know. God can do what God wants." But I can't help but think that this question, versions of which are as old as humanity, really is a question about what God is, in God's core. And I think we get it wrong.

We *think* of God as all-powerful, we *hope* God is all-loving, and we *say* he's all-wise to give God an escape hatch.

We live in a world where power is the be-all, end-all, and where security is the core need for which we most grasp. We want most for God, or at least someone, to be in charge; to think that there really isn't a master artist who is going to turn the trainwrecks in this world into a beautiful tapestry somehow is an invitation to despair. So we think of God first as an exponential version of the powers we know, like a king.

But we also know we need God to be loving, or else we're all in big trouble. So we hope that that's the case. You can put together evidence to that end, but frankly, it's pretty mixed. Even if you excuse God from all the evil that's directly wrought by our own free choices, there still seems to be a lot of leftover hurt in life.

So we decide that God must just be wise. God is powerful enough to pull all the levers, and God loves us, but things turn out horribly anyway sometimes because God's wisdom is such that what we think is horrible is actually exactly what we need.

This is pretty conventional, orthodox theology. It's just not very satisfying.

I think that's because we put the wrong aspect of God in the center. Let me argue that John gets it right in his Gospel and letters when he asserts, again and again, that God is first and foremost Love.

If what we want most, what we'd be willing to gamble everything on, is that God is loving, then what we hope is that God is also powerful. And as risky (and heretical) as that sounds, it also renders God's wisdom a lot more understandable. God is not a master orchestrator who is wise enough to see how all these off-key notes resolve into beautiful music. God is a loving parent, whose wisdom says only that love is worth the pain, that even when things work out horribly, it's better to have had the opportunity to love, even in the mourning that comes after, than to not be, and not love, at all. Our hope is only that the power that springs from that choice to love is enough to bend this wreckage toward redemption.

• • • •

Originally published September 2020

I shouldn't be here.

As I contemplate 50, the first birthday I will celebrate without a living parent, I have the same thought that has struck me on most birthdays of my adult life, but maybe with a little extra poignancy.

I shouldn't be here.

I can't speak for others, but for me, being born from an unwanted pregnancy before *Roe v. Wade* has meant living with the feeling that, had I been conceived a few years later, I would almost surely have not made it to Day 1. So Year 50 is something.

I spent the first two-thirds of my life thinking I must have been born for a reason, that I needed to live up to the opportunity of my nativity. It was a lot of pressure and I don't think it served me well. I tried to compensate for all those whose parents made other choices. It was too much.

In the last third of my life, I accepted that nothing I could do would justify my escape from the womb, and I learned that the best form of gratitude I could offer was to enjoy the day I had been given. It has certainly made it easier not to get worked up about piddly things, having a constant reminder that I shouldn't be here at all, anyway.

For the most part, I have left the pro-life fights for others. I love too many people on both sides of that divide, and there seems so little interest in mutual understanding and compassion there.

But I will offer this much. I hope most of the people who have gotten to know me would say it was a good thing that I was born, that their lives might have been a little diminished for not knowing me, had I not made it out to them. And I would suggest that we have missed the chance to meet many who would have been way more awesome than I'll ever be, had they been given the chance.

I will admit to this vanity: if someone once said, *"That this guy is here makes me wish we made it easier for people to choose life,"* that would be something.

If I haven't reached that threshold yet, well, there's hope in the next 50. And regardless, I am grateful for today.

. . . .

Originally published January 2019

In the Jim Carrey version of "The Grinch," he has a throwaway line that sticks with me. Cindy Lou Who has just said something sweet about the Grinch, and as he pats her off the screen he says, "Cute kid. BAD judge of character," before indulging in some shenanigans.

Was Jesus a bad judge of character?

I ask because in John 5:1-15, Jesus heals a guy, and you kind of wonder why. I mean, why THAT guy?

Jesus is in Jerusalem and goes to this place where, apparently, there's a pool that occasionally gets stirred up, and it's said that when it starts bubbling, whoever jumps in first is healed. There is a big crowd there, just hanging out, waiting for the bubbles to come, and Jesus walks up to a guy who has been sick – basically paralyzed – for 38 years. And Jesus heals him, which is as sweet as Cindy Lou Who.

But...

There are a couple of times in the gospels when Jesus asks someone what they want. Usually the answer is pretty obvious, and the person gets it right. Like, he asks a blind guy, "What do you want?" And the guy says "I want to see." Tough stuff.

Jesus takes it a step farther with this guy and asks him, "Do you want to be healed?" Which makes asking a blind beggar what he wants seem tricky by comparison. And the guy shanks the answer; he doesn't say "Uh, yeah." He says "Well, you see, I don't have any friends to help me, and I'm not quick enough to get into the pool in time to beat all these other guys..." He completely loses the forest for the trees. Imagine if someone dressed like the monopoly guy came up to me with a bulging wad of cash and said "Do you want a million dollars?" And I answered "Well, you know, I keep trying out for the Rays, but they say I don't throw hard enough, or have a secondary pitch, and I'm 53." It's an answer, but not really what he was asking, and it closes off some significantly better options.

Jesus heals the man anyway, telling him to pick up his mat and skedaddle. It's interesting, because a lot of Scripture scholars compare this guy to another paralytic with a mat in the synoptic gospels of Matthew, Mark and Luke. THAT guy gets healed because his friends cut through the roof of the place where Jesus was speaking in order to get the guy in front of him. THIS guy, he doesn't have any friends, as he tells Jesus. Which Jesus maybe should have noticed.

Since this happens on the Sabbath, and observant Jews were not to work on the Sabbath, this newly healed guy gets in trouble immediately for walking around, carrying his mat, just like Jesus told him to. When he gets stopped by the religious cops for working on the Sabbath, he blames the guy who healed him. At that point it is revealed that he doesn't really know who healed him. He didn't bother to catch Jesus' name.

Really?

If you're sick for 38 years and some dude comes by and heals you, don't you at least get his name? This is not the Lone Ranger here. He was not some Masked Man.

Then, somewhat surprisingly, the guy meets Jesus again, in the Temple, and Jesus tells him to shape up and quit sinning so nothing worse happens to him. And the guy responds by turning Jesus in – going back to the authorities and saying "Hey, you know how you busted me for working on the Sabbath and I told you it was the fault of the guy who healed me? That guy's name was Jesus." And in John, this is what sparks the movement to have Jesus killed. Maybe the idea of not sinning was an affront to him, so he turned state's evidence against his healer?

So... this guy is not bright, has no friends, isn't grateful, and isn't loyal.

The story (which, as an aside, shows just how well the author knew the neighborhood around the Temple, which had been destroyed by the time this was written) is clear that there were a *bunch* of people at this pool waiting to get healed. And Jesus chose this guy.

So, was Jesus a bad judge of character?

Maybe everyone else there was worse. It's certainly possible. This guy was no gem, but he wasn't actively conniving to kneecap the people in his way.

Or maybe this is *exactly* the sort of person Jesus comes for. As uncomfortable as I am with the notion that God miraculously heals some people in the clear face of the evidence that a lot of other people don't get that healing, here's what I can take from this guy:

He isn't able to rely on his own wits. I mean, he bought into a strategy that he could clearly explain would not work ("I'm not fast enough.") for 38 years.

He doesn't have connections. They say "A friend will help you move, and a real friend will help you move a body." This guy doesn't have one friend, let alone a real friend.

He isn't grateful for what he has or what he gets.

He isn't particularly loyal or faithful.

If that's the sort of person Jesus comes for, I guess maybe I'm OK with that. Because, for one thing, that's the sort of person nobody else is going to line up to help.

And for another thing, I can point to my own dim-wittedness, impotence, ingratitude and lack of faith.

Is Jesus a bad judge of character?

I sure hope so.

• • • •

Originally published September 2022

What a Hairless Mexican Dog Taught Me About Mercy

My first lesson in 2016, this Jubilee Year of Mercy, as it has been called by the Pope, came from a hairless Mexican dog and her owners over the New Year's weekend.

Chica, the dog in question, is owned by friends of ours. Over Thanksgiving, we house- and dog-sat for them, and my daughter, always passionate about dogs, bonded with Chica and her brother Taco.

On New Year's Eve, we got a text: Chica had gotten out. Our family was distraught, but only to a fraction of the distress of the owners.

Over the next few days, they literally didn't rest in their search for Chica. We helped a little – designing and distributing fliers, calling vets, posting on social media, hoping to mobilize other sets of eyes. On New Year's Day, someone called to say they saw Chica get hit crossing a major street, but that when the caller went to help her, she took off, as fast as any greyhound. We spent the night helping the friends comb the streets and alleys where she was last seen. No signs.

While I idled through the streets, what I couldn't shake was how this was a parable for our time. The shepherd with a lost sheep meets the prodigal father.

The unflagging devotion of Chica's owners – they could not rest until their dog was safe, and they would do anything to secure her — that's how God pursues each of us. And they were relentless.

And Chica? Her every need was met, she was showered with love and treats and an FSU T-shirt, and when she got the chance to leave all that, she bolted. Driven by fear or longing for something she thought was better than the perfection she had.

That's us.

The owners never gave up hope, but on Saturday night they realized they had done everything they possibly could. Though their role in the parable was the divine one, they were only human, and they put things in God's hands and collapsed.

In the night, Chica came home, waking them at 4 a.m. with her kisses. She was bumped and bruised but no worse. In the end, as we all know, no matter how fierce the search party, ultimately you don't get found so much as you find home.

And the owners? They were thrilled beyond words.

That's what divine mercy looks like.

• • • •

Originally published January 2016

Like a flowering weed growing through the concrete, mercy finds a way.

Hey, here's something that surprised me about the Bible. John 8:1-11 has one of the most famous and oft-depicted stories in the New Testament: Jesus and the woman caught in adultery. This is where "let he without sin cast the first stone" comes from: Jesus comes upon a crowd that has caught a woman in the act of adultery, and they ask Jesus whether they should follow Levitical law and stone her to death, and he writes... something ... on the ground before telling the crowd that those who are sinless can cast the first stone, and they disperse, one by one, starting with the oldest. Finally, Jesus looks up from his doodling, asks the woman where everyone has gone off to, and tells her to go and not do this again.

You know that story, right?

It almost certainly wasn't an original part of the Gospel of John.

If your sense of Scripture is that it was handed down by the Holy Spirit directly to the guys who wrote each book, dictated verbatim from God, you might want to sit down.

Fr. Raymond Brown's Anchor Bible Commentary is my go-to source for this, for those who might think I am prone to making stuff up. The earliest commentaries on John's gospel, and the oldest manuscripts of the gospel, don't include this story, as compelling as it is. From a storytelling sense, it breaks up the narrative pretty awkwardly. And linguistically, it uses a lot of language that fits well in the other gospels but sticks out like a sore thumb in John. In fact, there are some pretty old manuscripts that have this story stuck into Luke 21 instead, though it almost certainly wasn't originally there, either.

There is some evidence that the story was floating around in the circles of early Christianity, and by the 5th century, in St. Jerome's Vulgate (Latin) version of the Bible, it had landed in this slot.

Basically, this is a story that wasn't a part of the original gospels, but was too on point to leave out.

I don't have any new wisdom to offer on the story itself. The themes of hypocrisy and mercy are so rich on their own, and many much wiser souls have said plenty about this beautiful, short story. (I will add that it struck a chord that the oldest members of the crowd were the first to give up on the lynching; the older I get, the harder it is for me to hold on to self-righteousness.)

But the fact alone that it somehow got snuck into the Bible and made it this far encourages me plenty, even if it's unsettling for some. While it has some points of commonality with the Apocryphal story of Susanna in the Book of Daniel, with a woman accused of adultery, this story doesn't ever claim that the accused was innocent. It just leans into the reality that none of us have clean hands, that we all rely on mercy and forgiveness, so we ought not be slow to offer the same.

Pope Francis once called a special Jubilee Year to celebrate mercy, and put his name on a book called "The Name of God is Mercy." My guess is, if he goes down in history as "the pope of mercy," he'd be OK with that. Because we need the reminder, often, that mercy is all we can put our hope in, just like the guys with the rocks in their hands. Or the woman they were aiming at.

I live in a place where almost everyone came from somewhere else, and the only thing they can agree on is that we should quit letting in so many new people, because of the traffic. And it takes the same hypocritical mindset to say that it's OK for me to experience forgiveness, but *now* we gotta start cracking down on folks.

That message of mercy sounds weak, but, man, it's gritty. It shows up at the most inopportune times, like at the sentencing phase of a trial. Like a flowering weed working its way through the pavement. It'll even worm its way into the Gospel when you're not looking.

. . . .

Originally published October 2022

Get To? Or Have To?

I think it was Bert and John Jacobs, in their book about their clothing brand *Life is Good*, who first flagged for me the fundamental difference in mindset that happens when we say we *get to do* something compared to when we say we *have to do* something.

Think about it: How different is it to say "I get to go to work today" than "I have to go to work today?" "I get to work out today" versus "I have to work out today?" You can change your life just by swapping those phrases out.

Maybe the biggest barrier to making peace with yourself and with God is that we put love on the wrong side of ethics. We think about peace, or happiness, or acceptance, as something that we can only find after we do a bunch of "have-to" things. For a lot of people, that means keeping commandments (which by their very nature are "have-tos") or measuring up to all the other norms and rules and unspoken expectations of what a "good person" does. For others, it means accomplishing some great calling or mission (which I can verify is every bit as much of a trap). Only to the degree that you do those "have-tos" do you get to feel peace, happiness, God's love. And, unless you're a lot different from me, it's way easier to see where you don't measure up than it is to see where you do.

The Church is fully complicit in this. This might be true with most culturally dominant religions, come to think of it. From an anthropological standpoint, religions exist to enforce a social order, a code of have-tos. So kids come out of church schools steeped in guilt and well-versed in the have-tos. From the outside, what religion has to offer is a transaction: Do the have-tos, and you will get to heaven someday.

That is a sucker bet. As a result, people either leave religion, content to enjoy the single marshmallow of this life's empty pleasures instead of holding out for the promise of two marshmallows in the great beyond, or they get trapped in the endless web of have-tos, always feeling like they don't quite measure up, that they're down 12 late in the fourth quarter of the game.

We need to root that approach out of our way of being, because it is the opposite of the Good News.

Think about a loving relationship you are in, or have been in. There are a million things I do for my wife, or my daughter, or even a lot of people I'm not related to, that you could never *make* me do as part of a commandment structure of have-tos. You could not compel me to change diapers for the promise of heaven or the threat of hell, but I've changed plenty of them for love. I have endured any number of things I did not enjoy, and volunteered for any number of tasks I would never do for myself, because by doing so, I helped make the life of someone I loved just a little bit easier. I didn't *have* to, but because I loved, I *got* to.

I think that's what we Christians get wrong about this thing we profess. The institutional instinct of the religion is to focus on the ethics, to make sure people do right, so we end up pushing ethics out of order. In the process, we lose the essence of the Gospel.

We are loved immeasurably by the God who made us.

Full stop.

No "if-then" statements. No "have-tos." All we profess:

- The Incarnation – that God stooped to become one of us because He wanted to be with us *that* much.

- The Eucharist – that God wants to be *in* us and *with* us in a way we can't even wrap our heads around.

- The Crucifixion – that God would endure anything to be with us.

- The Resurrection – that God shows that even the worst we can throw at Him is not enough to drive him away.

Those are all totally insane things that God didn't have to do; God would say God *got* to do them, because that is what love does.

(Another day I'll say more about how that points to the real reason why marriage is a sacrament; because it invites us to mirror that mutual self-sacrificial love, to the extent that we get to offer it to each other.)

When people asked Jesus what have-tos to prioritize, what he said was, love God back. And love whom God loves, which is everyone, especially the outcast. By doing so, you'll be surprised at the things you get to do.

What the Gospel offers isn't a transaction, it's a relationship. What we don't say enough is, those ethics of love of God and neighbor aren't really have-tos; they are get-tos, in response to a God who loves us regardless of what we do or don't do. If we choose to love God back, we get to play on God's team in bringing love, joy and peace to the world. And if we really buy the offer of that get-to mindset, we can make peace with ourselves and with God.

Now, if you'll excuse me, the dog just proved yet again that she is not really housebroken and I have to clean it up. Get to clean it up, I mean.

• • • •

Originally published July 2022

There's a great podcast by America Media called *Imagine* that offers a series of guided reflections in a Jesuit prayer tradition in which you put yourself in the scene of a Biblical story. One season focused on the Christmas story, and it has allowed me to see in a new way stories that are so frequently told that they become like wallpaper, mostly unnoticeable backdrop. It's been quite a gift.

Two episodes resonate anew this year for me. In one, we are walking with Joseph and Mary as they leave their home, with Mary 9 months pregnant, to go 70 miles or so to Bethlehem to report for a government census. In the next, they arrive in Bethlehem, find no place to stay, Mary goes into labor, and they settle for a stable.

I know you know those stories, probably so well that you can't sink your teeth into anything new in them. At least, that was my reaction. But imagining walking along and talking with them, as Joseph packs up to leave, as they trudge along the long road, as a first-time mother manages a labor in filthy, stinky, foreign conditions, knowing the complicated backstory of this unwed couple, one thing was so powerfully clear:

This. Is. So. Messed. Up.

Traveling at 9 months pregnant. For a census. Giving birth in a stable without any help. With a fiancé who is not the child's father. Cleaning out a feeding trough for a bed. So messed up.

I'm not a Biblical literalist. Neither the infancy story Matthew tells nor this one that Luke tells needs to be factually accurate in order to speak truths, in my book. The census Quirinius actually called didn't happen when Jesus was in the womb, scholarship says; Luke might have had the facts wrong, or maybe it is just a device to get the Holy Family to Bethlehem, to align with the early tradition about Jesus and with Old Testament prophecies about where the Messiah was born. I am very comfortable with Gospel writers reverse-engineering a story that helps them set up the inexplicable experience of a Resurrected Jesus and what that means for us today.

But the magic of Luke's version of Jesus' story is how the ineffable is so closely interwoven with the irretrievably messed up. The Holy Family is an unwed pair of homeless laborers in a foreign town, and the first people who recognize them are from society's lowest rung, in a setting barely fit for animals (which, pre-21st Century urban America, is pretty awful).

Walking with them through the messed-up-ness — the hopelessness of packing for a really stupid trip, the desolation of being in a foreign place without a home or a place to turn, the birthing of a child into this pitiful scenario – this was a beautiful and hopeful experience in 2020, when so much of our lives seems so irrevocably effed up.

God is not only in that mess; God chooses that mess to say "Yes, even here. Especially here."

It is upending in a way that is hard to reconcile with the idea that the Gospel birth narratives are meant to be hagiographies.

And it made me chuckle, at the absurdity, as well as at the recognition that God is saying that yes, even here in 2020, especially here in 2020, the thrill of hope appears.

· · · ·

Originally published December 2020

Weird Family Dynamics: The Wedding at Cana Version

Sometimes I think we think of "The Bible" as this sternly monolithic statement by God about... everything, really, and we can forget that it's really an anthology, a collection of books written at different times for different audiences in different styles and for different purposes. Some of these books are either so clearly relevant to our lives or so transparent in their purpose that they seem pretty relatable. But most of them are not that straightforward, and when you slow down to think about the details of the stories they tell, some of them are a little odd.

John's gospel, for instance, is a lot weirder than it gets credit for. Because 3:16 gets put on posters at ballgames, I think it gets a benign pass by people, when a closer look shows some, well, quirks.

Take the Wedding at Cana. This is John 2:1-12, the first miracle (or Sign, as John calls them) that Jesus performs in John's gospel. It doesn't appear in the other gospels at all, but we have all heard the "water into wine" thing a zillion times. (Digressive shoutout to All Saints Cafe in Tallahassee, which had a T-shirt with Jesus on it saying "All Saints Cafe: Turning Water Into Coffee.")

But look closer. This story has some real quirks.

John doesn't name Mary, *in a story about Mary*. She is only "the mother of Jesus." And before you start, John has no problem naming names; he's the only one who names Malchus, the guy Peter de-ears in the garden of Gethsemane, for example. And Jesus just calls his mom, "woman." She's your mom. She has a name.

But what was Jesus' relationship to his mother like? Mary was invited to the wedding... and so was Jesus, separately, with his disciples, who have only been with him for three or four days. It seems a little off that their invites were separate, and his +1s were basically strangers.

When the wine runs out, Mary doesn't ask Jesus to do anything. She just says to him "they have no wine." To which Jesus basically eye-rolls back "O woman, what have you to do with me? My hour has not yet come." The shorter and more familiar version of which is "Mommmmmm!"

So John's 30-ish Jesus is apparently a teenage boy when his mom is around. Actually, that may be the most relatable moment of all four gospels for me. I have definitely lived that moment, even in adulthood.

You know (or can read) the rest of the story, but the bridge verse in 2:12 is also interesting: he leaves Cana for Capernaum "with his mother and his brothers and his disciples, and there they stayed for a few days."

Christians put a lot of weight on this wedding story. In some traditions, the reason weddings are a sacrament at all rests on the fact that Jesus performed his first miracle at one. Again, for John, this is the start of Jesus' wonder-working career. It is a big deal.

But the story isn't about the wedding. It's about a party running out of wine. There's no mention of an actual ceremony, religious or otherwise, and the couple doesn't actually appear. And as miracles go, water-to-wine seems very... parlor tricky. Nobody gets raised from the dead or healed or exorcised, and those are all really serious. Here, the party gets to continue.

I'll say this, though. It's a miracle that casts light on the little things that are more important than the serious things, maybe. Whatever comes of it, a wedding is a celebration of joy and hope, and in a world that is short on both, those things can be written off as extras, grace notes, bonuses.

Joy is important. Hope is important. Letting a celebration run its full course is undervalued, now, and maybe then. We need to do the hard work of love and justice, but it's better work when it starts and ends with joy and hope. So, yeah, 150 more gallons of wine all around.

Father Mike Schmitz gave a great homily on this passage once. He noted that Jesus, through this trick, turned a moment of shame that would always follow this couple (running out of booze at your own wedding) into a moment that would make them legendary (who saves such great wine for last?). This little trick might have changed the trajectory of that couple's life for the better. That's kind of sweet, and replicable in other graceful ways.

But as someone who rolled his eyes, figuratively and literally, at his mom's entreaties well into alleged adulthood, maybe the miracle is in that bridge verse. If our relationship with our kid is so strained that we don't show up on the wedding invite list together, if they show up with fishy-smelling randos that we've never met, if they call us, not "mom/dad" but "woman/man," and if they react to our request for help with an epic teen eye roll, would it not be a miracle of a strange but treasured sort if we got to leave together with them, and he let us join his rando friends for a few days down by the coast?

John's gospel is quirky and abstract and poetic. But if you look close enough, it's also beautiful and real.

• • • •

Originally published June 2022

Falling Apart

Since the late '90s, I really haven't watched traditional fiction TV series. But back in the era of Must See TV, shows like *ER* always had these crazy season finales that would be spectacular in the scope of their drama. People would die, people would move on, people would disappear, and you would be left for the summer wondering how on earth the story would continue in the fall. Maybe that model of television storytelling still happens; I'm not sure. (Streaming series are a different bird.)

The last couple of weeks have felt like a season finale. Sure, in our own tiny world, the kid going to college is one of those big transitions (so far, all good, and not what this post is about), but I have a shocking number of close friends who have experienced tragic losses, others who are facing scary diagnoses, and on top of that, we've got hurricanes, wildfires and pandemics, and an undoing of 20 years of war abroad. Even compared to the last 18 months, it feels like a climactic finale. Whatever next looks like, it'll be really different.

During the lockdown portion of the pandemic, I got to watch the *Harry Potter* and *Star Wars* movies (yeah, that was a loooong lockdown, wasn't it?), and one thing that jumped out was that, in each of the sagas, the general vibe was that the world was falling apart. The victories in both series weren't so much triumphs as miraculous survivals. Even when you blow up the Death Star, the Empire still outguns the rebels and the emperor still lurks. Even when you survive Voldemort, he escapes, sometimes stronger.

When I was in college, one of my religion classes focused on the Tolkien *Lord of the Rings* books. When I was in seminary, I had a lot of classes infused with theology about the brokenness of the crucified Jesus. The throughline, really, was from John 1:5: *The light shines in the darkness, and the darkness has never put it out.* The world is falling apart, and God is in the fact it is still around at all.

When I was younger, I wanted none of that. I wanted the triumphant God, not the loser God who barely makes it out before the explosion. I expected victory, not just the avoidance of defeat. This dark worldview where the miracle is that we are only "mostly" defeated? Not having it.

Sometimes non-Christians scoff at the Christians who seem to have their heads buried in the sand, convinced that there is a (literal) *deus ex machina* coming soon in which the good guys triumph and the bad guys are vanquished. You look around at the world, you look back on the good people who died too young and the people you love who you wanted more time with and the dreams that didn't happen, and you know that the story doesn't end tidily, wrapped in a pretty bow.

But to the extent that life experience has given me the wisdom I didn't have as a twenty-something seminarian, it has taught me that the world has *always* been falling apart. Ever since Adam and Eve ate the apple, if you will, things have been going south. The world was falling apart during the long span of Hebrew Scriptures. It was falling apart when Jesus was led to the cross, and it was falling apart during the first three centuries of Christianity, when Roman rulers martyred believers in spectacularly gruesome ways. To the extent any of that has changed since then, it is because we have cropped the photo to exclude the majority of the world, where children die young of preventable disease, war rages, famine reigns, and good people get gunned down in their prime while people we love get fatal diagnoses.

The world is falling apart. Just like it ever was. But somehow, against all odds, the light still shines, and the darkness has not put it out. Next season's premiere may be really different, but it has already been greenlit and is in production.

· · · ·

Originally published August 2021

Have you ever thought about the fact that, if a student dies while they are away at college, their parents have to go pack up their stuff? If you can imagine a mother or father pulling the clothes of their just-passed child out of the drawers of the dorm room dresser (or, more likely, pulling them off the floor) and packing them to take to a now-empty room at home, can you do anything but ask:

Where is God in this?

Or for those less God-inclined:

Where is Love in this?

I find this question really helpful. Sometimes it's a lament, but more often it's like one of those "Where's Waldo?" puzzles that were big a couple decades ago, where the question invites you to stop and look at the easy-to-miss angles, looking for love to show up in the mundane or the terrible.

While we were visiting my daughter at school, we attended a "celebration of life" for one of her classmates, Pato. They weren't close, but they were both second-year theater majors, and she was stage-managing a festival of student-written works that included one of his creations. He was in an accident the week before it opened and died a few days later. The school debuted his work for his family and friends the evening before the festival, and the celebration of life was the day after the run of the festival.

That was hard to find God in. My daughter said she saw a father doing laundry in her dorm, and thought for a second he looked like Pato's father. The thought of a father and mother packing up their son's room forever while everyone around them is just packing up for summer break was too awful to sit with.

So where is Love in all this?

At the service, Pato's father spoke to the pain and emptiness of what he and Pato's mother were going through. And then he talked about how the community — not just their family, but the school community of students and faculty and staff and administration and other families — had wrapped them up in love and support and shared memory. So, Love was there.

And before that, Pato's roommate and best friend (and already, at 20, a C-list celebrity) sang a song he and Pato co-wrote about seizing life in a way that only 20-year-olds can sing. Maybe he or one of the others in Pato's "We're going to make it big" crowd of close friends will use Pato's death as inspiration to do something special. Love would be there, too.

I have discovered that not everyone has this experience, but when I am around death, it makes me think about my own mortality. *Memento Mori* is not only the name of the gift shop next to the Haunted Mansion; it's also a long Catholic tradition of remembering that you will die as a way of contextualizing your life.

That can be risky, if your mind goes straight to what's-the-point despair or you dwell in the depression of "Would as many people miss me as him?" comparisons.

But it can be good, too. Realizing that tomorrow isn't promised can help you savor today. Knowing death comes for us all can give some urgency to the important things you might be tempted to put off.

Yogi Berra allegedly said "Always go to other people's funerals, otherwise they won't come to yours." If you can focus on who would miss you if you were gone (instead of who wouldn't), it can be kind of a scoreboard of love's legacy. And if your imagined funeral isn't as packed as you want it to be, maybe it's a nudge to make the world a little better, to offer a little more kindness, to make yourself a little more missable tomorrow. Love ends up in that, too.

I'm not a big believer in God "having a plan" that will "all work out in the end." Maybe I pulled a hope muscle or something. I resist romanticizing or excusing horrible things as part of a bigger beauty tied up in a bow.

But I do see the tiny beauties in the carnage, the almost invisible ripples of goodness that come off of the worst of times. I don't think it's a fair trade, but I do see that Love is there, if I look hard enough, as the remnant in the wreckage that lives to love another day.

Look, none of that is going to help you when it's your kid whose laundry you're gathering in the first moment of their absence. Nor is it going to "balance out" in some way that you see in years or decades to come. All I can hope is that the looking-for, and the occasional finding, of love writ small counts just enough to keep going.

Good Friday God

We want the God of Easter, an all-powerful God who conquers death.

We want the God of Emmaus, an all-knowing and wise God who can explain how in the grand plan this wreckage makes righteous sense.

But sometimes what we get is the God of Good Friday, an all-loving God who hurts with us rather than try to explain or fix, not play-acting but fully experiencing the loss that loving deeply always risks.

The God of Good Friday doesn't have a lot of competition in the marketplace of idols and ideas. Power, righteousness and omniscience have a lot more shelf appeal than vulnerability and suffering.

But it's the Good Friday version of God that truly leads with Love and opens the door to Joy and Peace, even if they share space with Sorrow and Ache.

Seek that God, the God that runs contrary to the superhero deity type. Good Friday is always just around the corner, and you'll want company when it comes.

• • • •

Originally published April 2022

Why Are You Looking for God?

I've been mulling this question a lot, from the perspective of what draws different people to religious belief. It's a rephrasing of a question at the center of two chapters of the Gospel of Luke (7-8), which is a meaty set of healings and sayings between some better-known events, the Sermon on the Plain (where the Beatitudes come from) and the commissioning of the Twelve Apostles. In the middle of this small whirlwind of well-told and well-known stories, Jesus stops to ask the people, when they went to see John the Baptist, "What did you go out to see?" He asks it three times in quick succession, so it must have been a question that was really important to Luke, the author.

Rightfully so, because Luke's Jesus talks about John the Baptist as a true messenger of God. And what we're looking for, when we're looking for God, tends to shape what we see. I was thinking about that, not in terms of people in Jesus' time going to see John the Baptist, but in terms of why people today go looking for God.

(We're all different people shaped by different experiences, so our answers are going to be different. There are folks who try to put those different expectations into a developmental hierarchy; while I understand what they're trying to do, I can't help but notice that the people at the top usually think like the person making the hierarchical model. I also can't help but notice that people at every level of the hierarchy seem to show the effects of a true encounter with God. So I don't mean this to sound hierarchical.)

Some people look for God because they're scared. I think mostly of people who are scared that they are going to go to Hell if they don't get on God's good side, so they are looking for God to show them what they need to do to "go up rather than down" when they die. Anyone who has lived in a culture of punishment, a family or friend-group whose love was conditional, or a work tribe that only offered approval to those who didn't screw up, knows this mindset. I'll just say that that's not a motivation that speaks loudly to me, but I know people who seem to live holy lives and are kind to others who seem to be driven by fear of God's wrath and desire for God's approval.

Some people look for God because they want to be part of something bigger than themselves. I've seen more than a few times over the years that among the essential things for human flourishing are belonging and purpose. And I think that today's world offers way too little for people in either category; even before the pandemic, we were isolated, and many people say that their lives are tough to find meaning in.

There are a lot of places where you can claim to be part of something bigger than yourself, that you can be caught up in transcendence. Frankly, that's the story of modern sports fans. When I took sociology of religion and read about religious rituals from an anthropological perspective, the purest example I could think of was a big-time college football game. We lose ourselves in a larger collective as a sports fan, even if it's ultimately not very purposeful.

Conversely, modernity offers myths that provide a story of greater purpose and meaning to which we can attach ourselves. Having just finished the full Star Wars saga, that one is fresh in my mind; the Harry Potter universe is another modern example. But even in (sort-of) real life, a lot of the storylines that swirl around our political world today carry this air of ultimate meaning, and if our day-to-day seems kind of meaningless, those storylines are attractive in their claims to purposefulness.

Ultimately, though, it's the nature of the story of God's love affair with God's Creation that provides insuperable meaning, and joining a community of fellow believers, however you define "community," grounds belonging in that ultimate meaning.

There's a third way. (Spoiler: with me, there is almost always a third way.) Maybe it's not about fear or about belonging and meaning.

Maybe some people look for God because they want to be fully and intimately known. I started to say this was "for love," but love is so broad a term that it is insufficiently precise. It's the feeling of being accepted in the midst of total vulnerability that is the aspect of love I'm talking about.

Just like there are human analogues to faith that's based on seeking approval, and faith that's based on seeking belonging, so with faith that's based on seeking intimacy. We have experienced it, or experienced its lack, in our closest relationships.

I am stymied to the point of surrender by the divisions among people who profess belief in the same God. I was driven to this meditation by the gnawing need to understand how we can be so far apart despite God's clearly stated desire that we all be together. The hypothesis of the day, for me, is that we are all approaching the same God, but our answers are really different to the question "Why are you looking for Me?"

· · · ·

The thing about Luke 7-8 is it's one big double-down on the Lukan message that the outcasts are who God is here for. Consider the healings: an occupying foreigner and his slave, a widow, tax-collecting sellouts, a sinful woman, the disciples (who included self-professed sinners and tax collectors), a man infested with demons, a ritually unclean woman. Only the last healing, the raising of the daughter of a synagogue official, would have been seen at the time as being about someone who was "good people."

The funny thing is, when Jesus starts this healing streak, word spreads that Jesus is a great prophet who "has come to save his people!" (7:16) They're right, but they might have been surprised by which people God was claiming as his.

When John the Baptist's disciples come to ask Jesus if he is The One, here's what he tells them to take back to his cousin:

- The blind see
- The lame walk
- Lepers are clean
- The deaf hear
- The dead come back to life
- The Good News is preached to the poor

We can look at these (except maybe the last one) as challenges that medical technology is rapidly solving. We miss the point. The folks he lists, they're all outcasts in that society that are considered good for nothing, people who don't count at all; Jesus' message isn't about health care so much as it is the restoration to dignity of those on the outside. That's Luke's message throughout Luke and Acts, and it's really, really strong in this section.

• • • •

Why are we looking for God?

Maybe it's out of fear, or out of loneliness, or out of a need for meaning, or out of a desire for intimacy. No matter what, though, it is a reflection of our experience as spiritual outcasts, broken and incomplete. That's very clearly who Luke's Jesus is here for.

• • • •

Originally published September 2020

I wouldn't go.

There are bumper stickers around the Tampa Bay Area that say "Terry Would Go". They're a tribute to Terry Tomalin, who was the outdoors editor for the *St. Petersburg/Tampa Bay Times* and by all accounts a force of nature. I have friends who were close to Terry and are still deeply affected by his life, but I only really knew him through his writing. He was a life-loving, adventurous, kind soul by all accounts. The bumper sticker is inspired by a similar phrase, "Eddie Would Go," said of Hawaiian surfing legend Eddie Aikau, whose spirit was said to be similar.

In the New Testament, the four gospels (Matthew, Mark, Luke and John) all approach the story of Jesus in different ways, even if they mostly agree on the basics of his life. One theme in the Gospel of Luke is Jesus going off by himself to pray. It's worth noting that woven in two of Luke's chapters (5 & 6) there are several retreats that Jesus makes. In 5:16, amidst stories of large crowds gathered to experience the healing he offers: "But he would go away to lonely places, where he prayed." Before calling the apostles, "Jesus went up a hill to pray and spent the whole night there praying" (:12). When he comes down, he picks his twelve, settles on a level place, and delivers the heart of his message. It's all packed in, in 6:20-42; you can just sit with those verses for a lifetime and keep finding ways forward.

Who is Jesus here for? Look at the Beatitudes in Luke's version:

- The poor, and not the rich.

- The hungry, and not those with enough to eat.

- Those who weep, and not those who laugh.

- Those who people hate, reject, and insult, and not those whom people speak well of.

There's a reason that Simon Peter, Jesus' first draft pick, asks Jesus to leave him alone, because Simon knows himself well enough to know that he's a sinner (5:8). There's a reason Jesus parties with Levi the tax collector, telling the folks who stay outside, judging, "I have not come to call respectable people to repent, but outcasts" (5:32).

It's either innately human or thoroughly American that we can always see ourselves as the outsiders. If you don't think too much about it, that message of victory for the underdogs sounds like a fun one to deliver. But if I were up on the mountain or in the lonely place praying, I wouldn't go.

In 6:46, after he lowers the boom on the life he has in store for these blessed poor, hungry outcasts, Jesus says "Why do you call me 'Lord, Lord,' and yet don't do what I tell you," and no truer words did Jesus ever speak. If we actually listen to what Jesus wants of us, we know he's talking directly to us. Want examples? Here's what he says is the heart of his ethical message (6:27-42):

- Love your enemies.
- Do good to those who hate you.
- Bless those who curse you.
- Pray for those who mistreat you.
- If someone smacks you on the cheek, let him hit the other one, too.
- If someone takes your coat, give him your undershirt too.
- Give to everyone who asks you for something.
- When someone takes what is yours, don't ask for it back.
- Do not judge others.
- Do not condemn others.
- Forgive others.

(This is not one of those social media quizzes where you write in the comments how many you got right. Thankfully.)

Here's what *doesn't* count to God as good enough:

- Loving those who love you.
- Doing good to those who do good to you.
- Lending to those who will probably pay you back.

(And I'm not sure I'd do that well on those, either.)

If I had to choose between staying in a lonely place with just God, and going into the crowd and delivering this message, knowing that people wouldn't do it, maybe even knowing how this would end, I wouldn't go. I'd say, Hey, Father, I think imma stay here with you. Because going to preach this message to a crowd that won't take it seems like a waste of time.

But God's ways aren't our ways. Jesus would go. And he reminds us, the slow-to-leave, that not only should we go, too, but that it's never too late to dig into this life. "For He is good to the ungrateful and the wicked" (6:35). Jesus says that as a reason for us to be as merciful as God is, but it's also a good thing to remember when we would rather stay in the lonely spot and let the world fail on its own.

* * * *

Originally published September 2020

Unpaint the Rock

O ne of the things I noticed during the 2020 Pandemic Virtual College Tour is that several of the dozens of schools my daughter and I virtually visited share a tradition of painting a rock. In one case, we actually visited a campus *in real life* that had a rock like this, but we saw lots of pictures of others on college campuses. They were remarkably similar, given that they were trumpeted as unique.

Here's the deal: big rock in the center of campus gets painted by student groups to promote their organization/cause/marriage proposal/whatever. Rock gets painted a lot, sometimes hundreds of times a year. Groups have to schedule with an office in Student Affairs as to when they get to paint the rock. The rock, essentially, has a social secretary.

When we visited one of these college rocks, we joked that, if you ever stripped all the paint away, you might find that the rock underneath wasn't big at all and might be shaped totally differently. It was the thousands of coats of paint that we were really looking at.

Our problem as Christians is that we have painted the rock. The essence of the Gospel is pretty simple, if profound: we are broken but loved unreservedly. Nothing can overcome that love even though it's a love we have not earned. What's asked of us, if we're grateful for that love, is to love back and love others, especially those who might be fooled into thinking that they are outcasts.

That's it. That's the whole rock.

But we have painted on a bunch of layers on top of that rock. About social norms and respectability. About politics and economics and culture. About what words to use and what clothes to wear and where to sit and stand and live. About what to do with our time and our money and our power and our planet.

Now I'm an optimist, so I'll say that I think that all of those things started out as corollaries to the foundational message, the rock. If you love God back, here's how you can show it. If you love other people, here's how you act. But at some point, you start rounding off the corners and go straight from claiming to be Christian to these corollaries, just like you start painting on top of paint that may really be on more of the sidewalk than on the rock. And in the process, we get to the point where we equate being a good Christian with only loving some people, not all of them, and with protecting the people inside the circle rather than inviting in the people who are left outside of it.

And here we are.

We Christians, faced by some pretty appalling examples of people claiming the same faith but committing some pretty unloving acts in the name of that faith, we need to own up to painting on paint. We need to commit to stripping off the paint and getting back to the rock.

Here's another perspective of this metaphor: painting the rock, at these colleges, started as an act of rebellion and ended up being co-opted into the institution. Surely it was vandalous undergrads who first painted the rock, in defiance of the administration and at risk of punishment. I bet what they painted wasn't even wholesome. But then it caught on, and the administration realized that alumni remembered painting the rock fondly in a way that encouraged donations, then the school leaders decided it was no longer a rebellion but a venerated tradition. And they gave the rock a social secretary, to make it orderly and avoid conflict and keep it all organized.

If rocks had memory (and I do not believe that they do), they would cry out, "That's not at all how this started."

God's in-breaking into normalcy looks more like rebellious vandalism than venerated ritual. That may be hard for a Catholic to say out loud, but it doesn't make it less true; in fact, I'll tell you that what draws me back to the rituals of the Church I belong to aren't the soothing predictabilities of rote tradition but the possibility that God sometimes shows up there in a table-flipping, life-changing way. Just as I go back to baseball games, not for the bucolic and predictable ritual, but for the very live possibility that I might see something completely new and amazing. Perfect games. Triple plays. Game 162 comebacks. Some nondescript player buzzing around the outfield like an airplane in celebration after sparking a miraculous win.

If we want to really expose ourselves to that vandalous rebellion, we need to strip the paint off the rock.

Here's one more metaphor of unpainting the rock. We spend a lot of our lives taking who we really are and what we really care about and adding on. The job. The house. The status. The image that we have it sorta all together. And if we do that too much, we forget what the rock underneath was really about.

While we may have to decide to strip the paint off the rock of our faith, collectively and individually, you should know that life will sooner or later strip you of the coats of paint you put on your core. It might be late in your years, but it might not be. Either way, we all eventually sit with Job and face the question of who we would be without all those coats of paint.

We need to do ourselves a favor and be preemptive. Unpaint the rock. It's more beautiful that way, anyway.

• • • •

Originally published January 2021

I was reflecting this week on what a blessing my friends who are agnostic or atheist are. I'll get to that in a minute.

Here's something I learned last week that was pretty interesting. The opening verses of the Gospel of Mark quote Isaiah 40: "A voice crying out in the desert: / Prepare the way of the Lord, / make straight His paths." The other gospels also cite this verse, and all of them use it to identify John the Baptist as that voice crying out in the desert.

But that might not be how Isaiah wrote it. Apparently, and this is hearsay on my part, the Greek translations of Isaiah frame it that way – that the voice is in the desert crying out – but the Hebrew is a little different: "A voice crying out: / In the desert, prepare the way of the Lord."

That changes things subtly, because while we can have the luxury of hearing "the voice in the desert" as that weird guy who ate locusts and honey in the middle of nowhere, the original is more challenging. That voice is crying out, "Hey, y'all better go out in the desert yourselves and start making things right." The John the Baptist-as-voice version is an invitation to a curiosity; the Hebrew is a work order for us to fulfill. And the desert, the wilderness, the abandoned scary places, are where the action is. When Pope Francis talks about a Church that needs to live "at the peripheries," he means we better go to work in the deserts of our world.

One thing I noticed about my friends who are outspoken about their nonbelief (which is an admittedly small but marvelous sample size) is that it's not really the Good News and its moral connotations that they are resisting. They generally buy into the notion that we are called to live out Love by showering it on those who need it most, the folks who are left by the roadsides of life, those stuck in a desert of our making or theirs. They intuitively accept the message of the Hebrew prophets like Isaiah.

What I hear these friends rejecting isn't so much God as it is the group of people who claim to be God's followers. Sure, by extension, they might prosecute a God who lets such hypocritical blowhards claim His name, but for the most part, it's the chasm of hypocrisy Christians (and our Church) betray in the distance between our words and our actions that they object to. At the heart of it, my non-believing friends are offended that those of us who should know that our calling is to build a way in the desert seem far more interested in staying in our temples and palaces. It's their indignation at our hypocrisy that feeds the belief that this religion stuff must be a fraud.

I appreciate that indignation; many days, I need its reminder, and other days, I feel it myself. Now, look, I know that it is often people of faith who give their lives at the peripheries. I know the schools and hospitals, the refugee resettlement programs and gang intervention initiatives, the prison companions and intentional communities with the addicted and ill and unhoused, that are peopled by folks driven to those deserts by their faith.

I recognize that the nuttiest thing about the God of the Good News is the depths of mercy that allows backstabbers like Judas and blowhards like Peter and misfits like Matthew to stick around, even when common sense would say that Jesus needed a roster upgrade. So the idea that the leaders of the modern Church would be hypocritical, misguided and sometimes monstrous, while unacceptable and awful, isn't all that off brand.

Even so, it's a blessing to have friends who stand outside belief but still hear that voice crying out. They remind me that I really should be getting to work in the desert, and a lot of times, they're already out there doing God's work themselves.

Is there a more poignant verse in the Bible than John 1:11? Especially in the Revised Standard Version. "He came to his own home, and his own people knew him not." You know that image of returning home unremembered and unrecognized is poignant, because it shows up in movies so often.

It's a Wonderful Life, of course (if I had to pick one movie as an emblem of my life, it would be that one); *Family Man* is another (an underrated Christmas fave, mostly for Don Cheadle's bit part). Tom Hanks' *Cast Away* has an element of this. But the movie analogue I want to explore here is the Warren Beatty classic *Heaven Can Wait*.

What must it be like for your home to forget you? To show up and have your people say, "No, that face doesn't ring a bell"? *Heaven Can Wait* has this device in which, no matter which body Beatty's Joe Pendleton is in, it's Beatty, as Joe, that the audience sees, while everyone else sees the person whose body he's taken over. And Joe has to convince people (really, just a couple of people), that he's not the guy they see; *he's JOE*.

I can imagine God nodding at this device. And while John the gospel writer is making the point about the Jewish people, God would nod today, too.

Because when you look at the story of God as told in the Bible, when you look at the message and example of Jesus in the gospels, and then you look at the collection of people who claim to be the Body of Christ, just like Jesus, a lot of times you have to shake your head. *It's not the same guy. It's just Leo Farnsworth or Tom Jarrett. It's not Joe. It's not Jesus.*

In *Heaven Can Wait*, Joe didn't have a love, really. In some respect, the poignancy of John 1:11 is more like George Bailey not being recognized by his Mary, or Kate not recognizing Jack Campbell, or Hanks' Chuck coming back from the desert island to find his Kelly moved on. But how much more must it hurt to be unrecognized, not only by your love, but by your creation?

Yet here we are. Read the gospels; heck, just stick with this verse (also from John), "Love one another." And then look around at the Church and the world. How could we convince anyone that we are who we claim to be?

In *Heaven Can Wait*, the late Jack Warden plays a character, Max Corkle, who gives me hope. He was close to Joe, and he catches enough of a glimpse of Joe in Leo (and Tom) to realize that it's still *him*, even if nobody else can recognize him. Even when everything about Leo (and Tom) screams "not Joe", Max somehow discerns that Joe's in there, somehow, sort of.

I guess my wish would be to have the eyes of Max Corkle. Because there's a lot in the Church and in the World that screams "not Holy," "not God," "not LOVE." It would be a good assignment to go through the day squinting at people like Max, to find the Holy inside that nobody else can believe and the Love that nobody else can notice. Because nobody should be unrecognized at home.

• • • •

Originally published May 2022

Love is a whisper, necessary even when it is insufficient.

Sometimes threads converge to form a pattern worth noting.

Early this week, a good friend and committed advocate for justice sent me a quote from Sister Helen Prejean, the advocate for abolishing the death penalty who wrote the book *Dead Man Walking*. It said:

"It took me a long time to understand how systems inflict pain and hardship in people's lives and to learn that being kind in an unjust system is not enough."

She's right, of course. Anyone who has dealt with a truly kind customer service agent in a system in which they can't actually help you knows as much, to cite a common if trivial example. An empathetic executioner doesn't excuse an unjust death sentence, to cite a more significant one.

But kindness ain't nothing, either, I thought at the time.

Catholics (like Sister Prejean) are called to pursue love of neighbor both through personal charity and through the pursuit of a justice that honors the essential dignity of every single person (as well as that of creation as a whole). One way we get this wrong is by making this an either/or proposition.

This week, I read a chapter of Fr. Ronald Rolheiser's *The Holy Longing* that was on a spirituality of justice and peacemaking, and he made exactly this point. Part of his argument is that, too often, those who engage in the quest for justice on behalf of the marginalized lose sight of the goal, a vision of "justness" and wholeness that includes all of us in loving relationship, including our enemies. When we forget that, it's too easy to get sucked into the mindset of our opponents, and we slide into a "win at all costs" fueled by self-righteousness that closes off compassion for the other side and more or less ensures that the battle never ends. Our goal as followers of Jesus, Rolheiser says, is "not to win over our enemies, but to win our enemies over." And that approach doesn't happen without kindness, as far as I can tell.

But what does that look like?

Before I got around to the Rolheiser chapter this week, I detoured into *Forgive Everyone Everything,* by Fr. Gregory Boyle, S.J. Maybe you know who Greg Boyle is – the Jesuit priest who founded Homeboy Industries, the largest gang intervention program in the country. I've pushed his three wonderful books, *Tattoos on the Heart, Barking at the Choir*, and *The Whole Language*, enough that it's reasonable to ask whether I'm on commission. (I am not. Though I'm not opposed to it, Greg.) *Forgive Everyone Everything* is a compilation of 52 excerpts from those books, paired with original art by Fabian Debora, Executive Director of Homeboy Academy and a former trainee at Homeboy.

This week, the excerpt was called "Opening Fists," and here's what it said:

> *I've learned from giving thousands of talks that you never appeal to the conscience of your audience but, rather, introduce them to their own goodness. I remember, in my earliest days, that I used to be so angry. In talks, in op-ed pieces, in radio interviews, I shook my fist a lot. My speeches would rail against indifference and how the young men and women I buried seemed to matter less in the world than other lives. I eventually learned that shaking one's fist at something doesn't change it. Only love gets fists to open. Only love leads to a conjuring of kinship within reach of the actual lives we live.*

That sounds hopelessly naive, coming from anyone other than someone who has spent the last 35 years living with gang members in East LA, offering Mass in some two dozen penal institutions in the area, and burying several hundred victims of gang violence while serving and living with thousands of other former gang members who have participated in that same violence. The throughline of Boyle's outlook is to create a circle of kinship such that nobody stands outside of it. And it is through that lens that he and Homeboy not only build up the community of former gang members but advocate for policy changes that address the injustices that create a world in which gang membership is ever attractive to begin with.

That same week, the Psalm that was read at Mass included

Kindness and truth shall meet;
Justice and peace shall kiss.
Truth shall spring out of the earth,
And justice shall look down from heaven.

And the Old Testament reading at that Mass from 1 Kings is that of Elijah climbing Mount Horeb to meet God, not in the howling wind or crushing rocks or earthquake or fire, but in the tiny whisper.

That whisper, that is so easy to miss but is more powerful and essential than all the fireworks nature can offer, is Love itself.

When you think about that day's Gospel reading, Jesus coaxing Peter to try to walk on water, maybe it fits, too. If Jesus is calling Peter, and by extension all of us, to pursue loving justice, walking on water is perhaps a good metaphor. Like Peter, people like Sister Prejean or Father Boyle seem to pull it off for a while. For most of us, also like Peter, we can make it a step or two in the right direction before we get distracted by the waves, lose our balance, and sink into the morass. We forget that true justice requires kindness, even as true peace requires justice.

Maybe, if, unlike Peter, we can tune out the waves, or, like Elijah, not fall for the earthquakes and winds and fires, we can hear the tiny whisper that is love, leading us to kindness and justice together. Because that is the only thing that will ever be enough.

Wheat and Leaven and Pearls

I t's really easy to see the weeds and way too hard to buy the pearl.

Let's start with the parable of the wheat and the weeds (Matthew 13:24-30), and the idea that God lets the bad grow with the good right now because to uproot the bad might take out some of the good, so He's going to sort it out at the end.

My wife is probably sick of me saying this to her, virtually every time we talk about whatever has gone wrong in the world this time: our central problem is that the way we build our culture is around the false belief that there are two types of people: good people and bad people. Wheat and weeds.

And the reality is, the line of demarcation isn't between people but within each of us. If Fr. Greg Boyle can work 30+ years with Los Angeles gang members and he's never met a person who was evil, I think we've got to listen to him. And if we are brave enough to confront who we really are, it's easy to see the weeds within our own hearts. I know the weeds in my life are growing as well as the weeds in my untended yard.*

In the same chapter is the parable of the pearl of great price (13:46), about how God's reign is like finding a pearl that is so valuable that we're ready to sell all our stuff to buy it. Now, I'd like to console myself with the idea that maybe the finder/seller/buyer is God, and not us, that God giving up everything to be one with us is the deity's way of selling power, glory and control for us, the pearl of great price.

I love that interpretation. It's beautiful. But most importantly, it lets me off the hook. Because if the pearl of great price isn't us, but God, and the person selling it all isn't God, but me, well. I mean, I've got a retirement to prepare for in a decade or so. I need to build up that 401k, not empty it. I *need* this stuff.

In between these parables are some others, including one about how a little leavening goes a long way. I've written before about how it

53

feels like the world is falling apart, and the fact that we've made it as far as we have despite the calamity of this world is the best miracle we're going to get.

The truth is, for whatever reason, today was one of those days when that little miracle — that there was any wheat at all, that we were still around at all, etc. — was just not enough for me. One of the questions I have queued up in my little weekly examen is "Where did you find hope this week?" and I backed off using that one this week, because, honestly, I don't know what answer I would have.

There's a writer whose work I really admire named Jim McDermott, who mostly writes about pop culture and occasionally also about God. His weekly newsletter (about pop culture, less so God) ended with these two paragraphs:

> *Real hope, existential hope, is when you have nothing to fall back on, nowhere good to go, so you run into the only option you have, because even if it is really, really bad it's still something, and you just never know where something may lead.*

> *I guess there's humility to hope, in a way. To hope is to acknowledge not only that I can't figure it all out on my own, but that what I see in front of me, what I believe is all that there is, is not necessarily all that there is. Who's to say there's not a life-saving gap somewhere ahead, or someone waiting to catch you when you leap?*

Maybe it's in that place that you sell whatever you have left for the pearl, that you trust the farmer not to pull up what might be weeds just yet. Maybe that's the leaven you need.

• • • •

*This interpretation is not Matthew's by the way. Astute readers will see that Matthew understands these gospels as very much a "good guys vs bad guys" duality. I'm relying more on lived experience by underscoring the divisions within us, though Paul speaks to this inner division (in Romans 7, for instance).

Mark's Desert

The Spirit drove Jesus out into the desert and he remained in the desert for forty days, tempted by Satan. He was among wild beasts, and the angels ministered to him.

This short passage from Mark's Gospel is all we get from him on the temptation in the desert that Matthew, Mark and Luke all put between Jesus' baptism and the beginning of his ministry. If you're willing to strip off the parts of the story that we hear in the other two synoptic Gospels and just take this one as it's written, it reads differently, and I think in a way that's both more personally relevant and more theologically valuable. Here's what I mean:

There is a kind of a primal narrative that we all know that plays out in Matthew's and Luke's versions, a sort of a quest/challenge story that sounds like it could have come from Greek mythology. It has a distinct flow to it: hero goes on journey (into the desert), journey ends with ultimate challenge (showdown with Satan), hero conquers challenge and wins reward (ministered to by angels) and is certified as a hero (on to ministry). This journey-challenge-reward order is something we see throughout literature, and it informs what we think about the world and, by extension, about God: we set our minds on something, we expect a challenge, and we place reward on the far side of the challenge.

Mark's desert isn't like that. Go check it again. The temptations from Satan, the ministering angels, and the wild beasts (which don't make the cut in the other two tellings) are all thrown together throughout the 40 days. If you're wondering, what prompts Jesus to leave the desert in Mark isn't completion of any challenge; it's that John the Baptist gets arrested, leaving a need for a new voice calling for repentance in John's place.

I find this telling of the Jesus desert story a lot more applicable to my life. For one thing, life seldom feels so cleanly organized as the quest model. Every day, there are wild beasts that distract from the important parts of life. Every day, the evil spirit peppers me with temptations to choose despair. Every day, messengers remind me that hope and love win, even when it doesn't feel like it in the moment. Heck, sometimes the wild beasts, tempter and angels all show up between when the alarm goes off and when I get out of bed in the morning. That jumbled-ness just resonates as more real than the quest narrative.

For another thing, when I look back on my life, a lot of times the 40-days-in-the-desert experience isn't so much a matter of tackling a challenge as it is a time of letting things simmer, like a good sauce or stew. I can identify a period of a couple of decades where, spiritually, it didn't seem like there was much going on with me that anyone could tell. The ingredients were mostly there, but they just needed to mix and heat and settle before I could do much with them, I guess. (That process continues, of course, even now that I find myself doing stuff like writing these things.) Those fallow periods may seem like gaps, but maybe they were really these kinds of desert experiences, where stuff was happening, but out of anyone's sight.

I also think this picture of the desert experience is truer to the Gospel. I've said before and will probably say again, that we put God's love in the wrong place a lot of times — on the other side of accomplishment. We think in terms of the Matthew/Luke versions of the desert as we approach life: *if* WE venture boldly out into the wilderness and *if* WE overcome our tempters, *then* God will take care of us.

That's all wrong, both because of the "if/then" conditional nature of how it defines God's love and because it keeps us in the role of the protagonist, the ones controlling the outcome. The Good News that Jesus comes out of the desert to preach is the opposite of this. God loves us all – those who beat the tempters and those who get beaten by them. And, thankfully, there is nothing we can do to change that. The Good News is to accept that this is the deal and try to live like we believe it.

Maybe for Lent, rather than girding ourselves for a 40-day quest, we could be reflecting on the wild beasts and tempters and ministering angels in our lives and wondering what God has simmering in our souls, out here in the desert.

. . . .

Originally published February 2021

Whose Voice Would You Recognize in the Dark?

The Acts of the Apostles is my absolute favorite book in the Bible, and by far the most entertaining. It's too bad that it doesn't get more attention; in Catholic Masses, it only gets used (for the most part) during the Easter season between Easter morning and Pentecost, and even then, it serves as the first reading in place of the Old Testament, kind of like the opening act at the concert that nobody remembers. And the Protestant and Evangelical churches I know tend to spend lots of time talking about Paul's letters and the Gospels, and maybe an Old Testament story sprinkled in here or there. They don't know what they're missing, either.

Acts chapters 12-13 aren't particularly memorable, plot wise, but all the humor and weirdness of Acts shows up plenty. We've got prisons and preaching and weird deaths and just flat-out humor all mixed together in stories you probably haven't heard before.

Acts 12 is bookended by King Herod, the Hebrew King of Judea. This is the one in the gospels who had John the Baptist beheaded and by some accounts interrogated Jesus before sending him back to Pilate in the Passion narrative. Stuff plays out differently for him in Acts 12.

Herod was a politician who governed by watching the polls. He started persecuting Christians, saw his favorability numbers go up, and ramped things up by killing one of the apostles – James, the brother of John, who along with Peter and John was in Jesus' innermost circle. The crowds loved that, so he arrested Peter next, with plans to finish him off after Passover. "Peter was kept in jail, but the people of the church were praying earnestly to God for him." (12:5).

Prison security appears not to have been a strength of this age. Not for lack of trying, honestly. Peter was tied with chains between two guards while other guards were on duty at the prison gate, so it wasn't like a total sieve in there. But, as happens throughout Acts, angels intervene. This time Peter is pretty sure he's just dreaming, as the angel says "Hey! Get up!" and the chains fall off and he gets dressed and follows the angel out of jail, past the guards, through an opened gate, and down the street. Then Peter wakes up to discover that it wasn't a dream and he is now an escaped prisoner.

So he runs to the place where his friends were holed up, and he knocks on the door, and a servant named Rhoda comes to answer it. "She recognized Peter's voice and was so happy that she ran back in without opening the door and announced that Peter was standing outside." (12:14) And they argue about it, while Peter stands outside, a wanted man, continuing to knock on the door in the dark of night.

I mean, c'mon. That's a cartoon-level funny scene.

Then, in one of the more random lines in Acts, when they *finally* let him in, he says "go tell James" (not the dead one) and then "he left and went somewhere else." No context on where, or why, or how far away, or how long. That's how the story ends.

There are a couple other points in this section, but let me circle back to Rhoda. I used to go to the same drive-thru place for coffee every morning. The staff were pretty consistent. And I could not for the life of me identify most of the regulars there by voice alone. (The speaker system was not the problem.) There are any number of people I care deeply about who can call me, and were it not for caller ID, I would have no idea who they were. Maybe I'm particularly bad about that. But it makes me wonder how much time Rhoda must have spent listening to Peter, to be able to pick out his voice from the other side of the door in the middle of the night.

• • • •

So Herod gets mad at all this and has all the guards killed and decides to go spend time out of town in Caesarea. Also no context on why —

was he scared that Peter and the angels would come after him? Was he just going on vacation?

While he's there, he gets mad at the people of Tyre and Sidon, and they come to make peace. He puts on a show for them, so much so that they say "this guy is so impressive that he must be a god!" And immediately God strikes him down. "He was eaten by worms and died," it says. Not because *he* said he was a god, but because the people around him said he was a god. If you live by the court of public opinion, you die by it, apparently.

. . . .

Acts 13 cuts to Saul and Barnabas trekking around, and they go to the island of Cyprus. On the far side of the island, they encounter a magician who tries to undercut them by talking them down to the governor. The magician is a guy named Bar-Jesus (which means "son of Jesus"), but also called Elymas. Saul also gets called Paul here, showing two can play at the multiple-name thing. Saul/Paul curses the magician and he goes blind immediately, and there's a poignant half a line here: "he (Elymas) walked around trying to find someone to lead him by the hand. (13:11) That, my friends, is loneliness.

The governor, no Herod, sees this and buys into what Saul/Paul is saying immediately.

Paul and Barnabas travel on and get to Pisidia and go to the synagogue, where the local leaders say, "Friends, we want you to speak to the people if you have a message of encouragement for them." Cue a 25-verse mega-sermon, at the end of which everyone invites them back, so that the entire town packs the synagogue the following week to hear these guys. The local synagogue leaders get jealous, so Paul and Barnabas move on to the Gentiles, who welcome them. Then the local leaders get that group stirred up too, and Paul and Barnabas get thrown out of the region. They roll with it and move on. And the report back home leaves everyone "full of joy and the Holy Spirit," even though it sounds to me like a series of rejections.

• • • •

Look, I'm not saying there's a tidy devotional point in these two chapters; I certainly don't claim that the author had one in mind. But I can't get the question out of my head about how Rhoda recognized Peter's voice, and maybe it wasn't that he had a lisp or anything.

Maybe the voices we recognize in the dark are the ones that speak a word of encouragement to us. Maybe the voices we recognize are the ones that can leave us full of joy.

And maybe the reason the magician in Cyprus goes from being super influential to someone who can't find anyone to lead him around in his darkness is that his message was the opposite of encouragement and he didn't think he needed to offer encouragement to anyone else. When he's in the proverbial dark, nobody recognizes his voice. Maybe Herod gets eaten by worms and dies for the same reason – he was so focused on himself that he didn't care to encourage anyone else.

If part of what we are shooting for is to be full of joy, even when the externals of the story aren't so great, then we could do worse than be encouraging at every turn. It shapes us for the better, and people might remember your voice fondly. Even if, for a minute, they sometimes forget to let you in out of the dark.

• • • •

Originally published August 2020

Back when I was a kid and wanted to grow up to be a basketball coach, one thing that sunk in was the importance of playing "away from the ball." When you have the ball in your hands, everyone is focused on you. But in order for a team to be successful, you need the guys who don't have the ball to move around with a purpose and make things happen. Otherwise, you get the "Jordan and the Jordanaires" Bulls who never won anything, instead of the 6-time NBA Champion Bulls that Phil Jackson coached.

This isn't restricted to sports. My favorite TV actor was David Hyde Pierce in his role as Frazier Crane's brother Niles in *Frazier*. He was not the star (or else the show would have been called *Niles*. Duh.) But when he was in a scene that was about someone else, if you looked out for him, he would invariably be doing something fascinating and funny. He was a master at acting away from the ball, if you will.

The section of the Book of Acts that runs from chapter 9 through 11 has the big stars of the early Church in it. This is Saul on the road to Damascus, plus Peter raises a woman named Tabitha (or Dorcas, because it seems like everyone in Acts has multiple names) from the dead, and Peter has a "come to Jesus" of sorts in a dream about including Gentiles.

But while Saul and Peter hog the spotlight, the guy who I find fascinating is Ananias. (This is not the same Ananias who falls over dead after withholding money from the apostles in Acts 5; this one is completely different. How popular must Ananias have been as a name back then? Why aren't more kids named Ananias today? Anyway, I digress.)

This Ananias never met Jesus, but he was a believer in Damascus who, as best we can tell, was a well-respected member of the local Jewish-Christian community there. He is minding his own business when he has a vision in which Jesus calls him by name, and he says, echoing Abraham, Jacob, Moses, Samuel, and Isaiah, "Here I am." Nobody else in the New Testament invokes that phrase.

So Jesus tells him that Saul is in town and has gotten a vision that a guy named Ananias is going to lay hands on him so that he (Saul) can see again.

Ananias tells Jesus that he has heard all kinds of bad things about Saul (which, according to the author of Acts, were true), but Jesus says "Go, because I have chosen him to serve me, to make my name known to Gentiles and kings and to the people of Israel. And I myself will show him all that he must suffer for my sake."

So Ananias goes to "Brother Saul," as he calls him, tells him he's there because Jesus sent him, and places his hands on Saul and restores his sight. Other than Saul (now Paul) retelling this story in Acts 22, he has no other role in the Bible. Absolutely nobody refers to this story as "Ananias plays the hero." He is following God, away from the ball.

Here's the inspiration I get from Ananias in his supporting role:

1. He owns his moment. That one time that God calls his name, he answers with the same words as the Hall of Famers. Here I am, Lord.

2. He talks to Jesus directly. He likely had not met Jesus in his earthly ministry, and yet when Jesus appeared in a dream, he didn't just grovel; he said, I hear you, Jesus, but this guy Saul is really bad news. Are you sure? That takes a level of comfort with yourself and your god.

3. When God lays out the plan that Saul is going to be a major character in God's story, Ananias doesn't try to pull focus. He could have said "Why pick Saul for all that cool stuff, when I've been on your side all along?" He doesn't sulk or show envy. He just says "OK then."

4. He turns on a dime. Ananias goes from being terrified of Saul to calling him "brother" in a verse or two.

5. He recedes into the scenery.

The main characters in God's story, as told by the Bible, are almost always the most unlikely. But they only shine because of fascinating supporting characters who play their role and disappear. There aren't a lot of churches, nor people, named for Ananias. But he knew how to be faithful away from the ball.

• • • •

Originally published August 2020

Who God is Also Tells Us Who God is Not

Before we move on, let me highlight the three themes from the reflections above about who I have experienced God to be:

- God is love, first and foremost, which we experience as mercy.

- God is with us, here, especially in the messiness of life.

- God invites us to love sacrificially and counter-culturally, not as a prerequisite but as a response to God's love.

This is not new. Some might argue that it is not complete, and maybe they are right. But it is central to the traditional understanding of the Good News.

So what?

As I look for the idols whose temples I need to abandon, what jumps out at me time and again are the ways that we who claim to be Christians, individually and collectively, have not only added on to this essential "rock" of faith but have created versions of gods that don't align with that Gospel at all. The gods that focus on what's wrong with us to the exclusion of what's right with us. The gods that limit who deserves love. The gods that prioritize respectability and conforming to good manners over fully engaging in the mess. The gods that choose pride in the institution over the risky life on the periphery.

Those are some of the idols that are inside the walls. We need to abandon those temples first.

But wait, as they say, there's more. Who God is also makes a claim on who we are. We are beloved. Broken, sure, but beloved first and foremost, which means our brokenness is not complete or irredeemable.

That makes some claims on how we treat ourselves and each other. If we are beloved, broken, and invited, all of us, then we can't give up on ourselves, and we can't give up on one another.

That's the theme of the next part of this book. We are beloved. We are broken. And we are worthy of the love anyway.

Who Are We?

On Sin, Love... and Sisters

Explanatory note: I was adopted as an infant by a wonderful family with four teenage girls. One of them, Sharon, suffered from alcohol and drug addiction through much of her life, beginning in high school. Later in life, she came back to herself, marrying a wonderful man and settling into a mostly quiet life. She suffered from a number of illnesses in her last years and passed away just before she was to receive a kidney donation from one of her sisters.

Today I had the honor and responsibility to lead a very informal service for my family in remembrance of my sister, Sharon. I'm not an ordained... anything, really, but it was a family-only thing at one of her favorite places, Whitey's Fish Camp outside of Jacksonville, and I was as qualified to lead a service as Whitey's was to be a church.* Thanks to a good friend who actually is a priest, I was able to draw on an order of service, readings, and prayers appropriate to the occasion.

But there's a slot for a homily. I reflected a lot about what I learned about sin and God's love from my sister and my family and thought I should share some of it here:

One of the old jokes I learned in seminary was about a new pastor who had finished his first sermon at his first church. He was standing in the back, being complimented by the congregation as they filed out, when an old guy grabbed his hand, pulled him aside, and said, "Son, a sermon should be about three things. It should be about sin. It should be about God's love. And it should be about half as long as what you just did."

Obviously, I don't need to tell a joke to warm up a crowd that is family. But that joke kept coming to mind, because as I reflected on Sharon's life, I realized that watching her from my vantage point really shaped my theology, my understanding of sin, my understanding of God's love. I'll shoot to keep this half as long as a sermon.

Because I came along much later than my sisters, I never really knew Sharon before addiction knew her, and I was still at home for some of the hardest years of her life, when she was on her own and out of control. Of course, I'm also blessed to have known her after that, and her marriage, which is my easy mental tent peg for when she turned her life around.

We get sin and addiction backwards in our culture. We think of addiction as being about doing a lot of sinning, a lot of bad stuff that makes God mad. I don't think that's right. Watching how Sharon struggled with addiction, I realized addiction, rightly understood, is the best way I can understand sin.

Sin, like addiction, is the fierce upstream current we have to fight against in order to move toward the light and be the best person we can be. In Romans 7:19, Paul talks about how "I do not do the good I want to do, but the evil I do not want to do," and that's the force of addiction as surely as it's the force of sin. Fighting that current takes a ton of courage, and let's not fool ourselves, we all face addictions. For some of us, they are invisible or socially acceptable, like judgmentalism or anxiety or achievement. For some of us, they are relatively benign, like caffeine or smartphones. For some of us, they are visibly destructive and bring the added current of physical chemical dependency, and they can create a sense of shame that tricks us into staying away from the very love that is the only thing that can help us. To push against that takes a courage we should all admire. That's what I saw in Sharon. That's what I understand about sin.

We get God's love wrong, too. A lot of people seem to think of God's love as something you have to earn, like he's an accountant that audits your moral books before paying out blessings. There are legalists who think that way even today, just as there were Pharisees in Jesus' day. Those legalists complain that a lot of *other* people today think of

God as just an easy grader; he's still a judge, in their estimation; but he's willing to let things slide if you show good effort. Those are both wrong; that's not the love I know.

I saw what God's love looks like when I was living at home and Mom and Dad were dealing with Sharon's wild days. I saw their pain. I saw how many things they tried in order to get Sharon back on track. I saw how much it hurt to realize that the nature of human agency is such that you couldn't *make* somebody want something, even if it was making your own child come back to who they really were. And I saw that, even when they tried "tough love," the "tough" never, ever drowned out the "love."

That's the love of God that I know. The love of a parent who wants to return a child back to who they really are and are willing to do anything it takes to make it happen. I learned that from watching Mom and Dad with Sharon. I know families who finally gave up, who cut their lost child or sibling out of the mix. But even when Sharon wasn't around, she always really was, and we were as happy to welcome her back to herself as the prodigal father welcoming back his prodigal son. And we are blessed — so blessed — that she brought her husband with her. This is a family full of marriages you can look up to, and theirs definitely is among them.

One more thing I learned about life from Sharon is resilience. There were some false starts, some rehabs that didn't take, and my assumption was that in staring down alcohol, it would be all or nothing, that if she ever fell off the wagon it would be to roll all the way back to the bottom of the valley, probably never to get back up.

Sharon had some down times; I think as much as she loved the holidays, they were particularly tough. But those times when she got tripped up, she kept getting back up and shaking it off, and that was a wonder to see. That taught me what resilience was.

I can't say for sure what happens after death. Christianity proclaims a Resurrection at the end of time, but we also talk about heaven right now. Either way, I believe that death completes the returning of ourselves to wholeness, peace and love by returning us to our source.

I picked the Gospel about the "Good Thief" who asks Jesus, while they're both being crucified, to remember him. And what Jesus says is "Today you will be with me in paradise." Today. With me. Paradise.**

I don't think Sharon had too far to go. Wholeness? She picked up the pieces of the brokenness we all share, and she made it into a whole. Peace? She may not have been perfectly peaceful, but she set aside the restlessness of her younger days. Love? As I said before, she was always the most loving member of the clan.

Last Sunday, our pastor talked about how we can only really love when we know we have been loved, and I know Sharon felt that. That is, if anything can be, the silver lining of the awful timing of her passing. On her last day, she got to soak in the reality that she was *so* loved that her sister would give up her kidney for her. May we all feel that much love on our last day.

· · · ·

*Side note: Should you ever go to Whitey's, do check out the hand-carved tribute to the late Jimmy Van Zant. It's not exactly a saint's icon, but it's the culturally appropriate equivalent.

**Father Greg Boyle has a great reflection on this in his *Tattoos on the Heart*. Go buy his book or donate to his ministry Homeboy Industries.

· · · ·

Originally published November 2017

What is a Human Life Worth?

I heard an economist in early 2024 talking about the dramatic effects that the COVID-19 pandemic-induced shutdown had on the economy, how the combination of closing off entire sectors of the economy fueled unemployment, the infusions of government aid fueled inflation and supply shortages, and how for those three years, the challenges we faced were all reverberations from that combination of slamming on the brakes and then punching the accelerator of the national economic engine. And throughout his entire explanation, his message was the same: How could we be so stupid?

What he did not acknowledge was that studies have shown that, without lockdowns, perhaps hundreds of thousands more people would have died of COVID-19. He did not argue that those lives saved were counterbalanced by other lives lost to the health effects of isolation or economic disruption. There is evidence that people *did* die for those reasons, though not in anywhere near as large numbers as those who would have died of COVID-19. Regardless, that was not his argument. He simply did not believe that self-inflicted economic disruption at the magnitude we experienced in 2020 could ever be seen as anything but stupidity.

Which made me wonder, what is a human life worth?

This is a question that policymakers seldom, if ever, acknowledge, but is part and parcel to their work. Are we willing to trade off rights to gun ownership in order to save lives? Are we willing to trade off preferences for fast commutes over safe streets in order to save lives? Are we willing to trade off higher taxes in order to fund programs that save lives? Are we willing to trade off control over property in order to provide others what they need to live? Government budgets, laws and ordinances, even company policies around customer and employee safety and benefits, all have implications that can save or cost people their lives. Some tradeoffs we gladly make without thinking. Some, we would never consider. Others, we debate. But they are all rooted in the same question: What is a human life worth?

The truth is, it depends. In our society, and every other society I am aware of, some people's lives are worth more than others. The efforts to highlight systemic inequalities center on the argument that our financial, social, cultural, political, legal and economic systems value some lives more than others. The opposition to those efforts, to at least some degree, reflect a concern by opponents that the valuing of lives is a zero-sum matter. If *those* lives start to matter more, then *our* lives will matter less. For other opponents of these efforts, the argument is simply that they, too, have been victims of inequalities that aren't being noticed by those fighting on behalf of other victims. They all agree, though, that these fights are about not only what a human life is worth, but which ones are worth more.

This extends between societies. Whether in debates on international relations, global trade, or immigration policies, policymakers are confronted with claims that some lives (usually *our* lives) should be worth more than other people's lives.

• • • •

Recently, two of my wife's colleagues lost their spouses. One died after a long illness, one suddenly. To those widows, their spouses' lives were worth everything. We would all say the same about our spouses, our children, our parents and siblings and friends. You cannot put a price on the life of someone I love, we will say. Their lives are worth everything.

But everybody is worth that much to someone. The Israeli hostage and the Palestinian child. The Ukranian soldier and the Russian. The refugee whose boat capsizes in the Mediterranean and the immigrant who dies crossing the U.S.-Mexico border. To someone, their lives were worth everything.

Of course, the same is true closer to home. The person who can't afford a place to live, the person who can't find a job, the person who needs to see a doctor, the person who just needs help getting through the day. Even the person we think was a jerk to us, the one who cut us off in traffic or got our order wrong or let their dog poop in our yard without cleaning it up, their lives are worth everything to someone.

If God is who God claims to be, all-Love, and we are who God claims we are, all-Beloved, then God is the someone for whom our lives are worth everything. This is the story of Creation, of the Incarnation, of Good Friday, of the Resurrection. Even the most isolated, outcast misfit is loved so much that their (our) life is worth everything. It cannot be measured in money or sacrifice or tradeoffs.

Our challenge is to live into that reality. Accepting that we are *that* beloved is hard, but it's the easy part. Seeing all the people around us, and knowing that they and all the other people who live beyond the horizon of our awareness are equally as beloved is the hard part. Accepting that reality puts so many claims on us, and calls into question so much of what our lives are built around. But that is who we are. Our lives are worth everything, and we are called to recognize that in each other.

Every day, maybe every moment, we ought to ask ourselves:

What is a human life worth?

The Lapsed Catholicity of Ted Lasso

" *Ted Lasso* is my new religion."

Since I got hooked on the AppleTV+ series *Ted Lasso* after its first season, I've witnessed the tidal patterns of word-of-mouth promotion that I guess is how ideas spread these days. Every few months, a friend on social media will ask a variation of, "Is Ted Lasso worth watching?" After one such inquiry, I responded with the comment, "*Ted Lasso* is my new religion," which was both goofily unserious and somehow not completely untrue.

I would argue that Ted Lasso, both the show and the character, has a lapsed Catholicity that refers back to both the outward signs and the deeper truths of faith, even as it/he claims an agnostic ground.

It's pretty clear that the show's creators have a deep familiarity with the mechanics of Catholic faith. You see the sign of the cross after a Star Wars/Catholic reference in the first episode of season 2 ("May the force be with you"; "And also with you."), between Ted and a character (whose son is a priest). When a character refers to a doner kebab place as "his church," a series of religious references ensue, including a joke referencing the Catholic doctrine of transubstantiation (how often do you see those?). In an episode set at a funeral, the characters discuss going to confession (which I'm not sure is a thing that Anglicans do.). When Coach Beard (a professed atheist) reveals that he has Vatican City citizenship, Ted makes the three-fold sign of the cross that Catholics make at the reading of the Gospel in mass. (Not to mention Dani Rojas' many references to Catholic spirituality.) These are small snippets in a non-religious show, but they are sophisticated enough to indicate that *someone* in the creative process knows what they're talking about.

But that's not really the Catholicity of Ted.

I should step back and say that there are some significant elements of the show that would offend many Catholics (and a lot of other folks). There is a LOT of swearing; Roy's first line in the series invokes the Holy Family in a curse and swearing is the *lingua franca* of most of the other characters as well. There is a fair amount of frank talk of sex outside of marriage as well as several plot lines that traverse that road. For many Catholics (and other Christians), the pervasive nature of these elements is disqualifying; I know many wonderful people who can't get past these things in a movie, show, poem or song. For some Catholics, the positive depiction of same-sex relationships is a stumbling block as well. Heck, Ted only refers to God in the feminine. In truth, God is rarely invoked at all.

But *Ted Lasso*, and Ted Lasso, retain an essential Catholicity.

Ted Lasso is, at its core, a show about the power of vulnerability and forgiveness in a wounded and broken world. As is the Gospel.

Jason Sudeikis, the show's co-creator and lead actor, has reportedly said that "this is a show about bad dads," and indeed, multiple character arcs revolve around the struggle to overcome the wounds caused by fathers, present and absent. In the penultimate episode, Phillip Larkin's "This Be The Verse" is quoted to Ted, and through it, the impact of the show's "bad dads" looks a lot like the Catholic doctrine of original sin.

But the show doesn't sit in that concupiscent swamp. A wounded healer with his own father issues, Ted brings a change in ethos within AFC Richmond that both affirms the essential dignity of each person, with special emphasis on the most outcast, and promotes a transparent embrace of mercy. Throughout the show, characters explicitly ask for, offer, and receive forgiveness, in dialogue more frank than what I experience in real life. The moments that most reliably bring tears in this show are those in which someone receives grace they weren't expecting. It is really something to watch.

The result of three years of this approach – a flawed leader focused on helping the group become their best versions while offering relentless encouragement, support and forgiveness – is a beloved community. When a player in season three says to the team, "I love you all so very much," it not only becomes a wordy rallying cry, but it just rings true. And the changes in character that result from bathing in that wellspring of forgiveness are truly inspiring.

So what? We Christians, of whatever stripe, stake our faith on the idea of an aggressively forgiving God in the face of our essential brokenness. We aspire to a community that reflects the grace its members receive. We invest our identities in the claim that the God who knows our failings still says "I love you all so very much." We proclaim that actually believing in that love can form us into better versions of ourselves.

As we in the Church try to grapple with a declining impact in the world, maybe *Ted Lasso*'s cultural resonance can remind us of some things. To the extent that we allow our faith to rise and fall on "traditional values," downstream ethics, and rules of decorum, we close ourselves off to the lives of others and brand religious faith as irrelevant to the culture.

But the core messages of the Gospel – the dignity of every person, the reality of sin and the power of mercy to overcome it, the offer to share our lives in vulnerable and healing ways – they still speak to the hearts of those who have wandered away. People are so hungry for those messages that they will watch a made-up American football coach in England just to see what forgiveness might look like. If we focused on the kerygmatic fundamentals of love and mercy, rather than fighting culture wars, could we get folks to recognize that they aren't just visible in fiction?

Maybe we just have to believe in BELIEVE, as the man says.

I don't like big crowds.

In big crowds, people are annoying, self-absorbed, and pushy. And by "people," of course, I mean me. I am at my worst in the midst of a big mass of disorganized humanity. Happy holidays.

Recently, I had a chance to step outside of such a crowd. I was waiting for someone, so I grabbed a seat outside the flow of the crowd and just people-watched. From that vantage point, they weren't so much a mass of humanity as a constellation of individuals with their own stories and challenges and beauty. It reminded me almost immediately of Thomas Merton's mystical moment at 4th and Walnut Street in Louisville, as relayed in his *Conjectures of a Guilty Bystander*:

> *In Louisville, at the corner of Fourth and Walnut, in the center of the shopping district, I was suddenly overwhelmed with the realization that I loved all these people, that they were mine and I theirs, that we could not be alien to one another even though we were total strangers. It was like waking from a dream of separateness, of spurious self-isolation in a special world. . . .*
>
> *This sense of liberation from an illusory difference was such a relief and such a joy to me that I almost laughed out loud. . . . I have the immense joy of being man, a member of a race in which God Himself became incarnate. As if the sorrows and stupidities of the human condition could overwhelm me, now that I realize what we all are. And if only everybody could realize this! But it cannot be explained. There is no way of telling people that they are all walking around shining like the sun.*

> *Then it was as if I suddenly saw the secret beauty of their hearts, the depths of their hearts where neither sin nor desire nor self-knowledge can reach, the core of their reality, the person that each one is in God's eyes. If only they could all see themselves as they really are. If only we could see each other that way all the time. There would be no more war, no more hatred, no more cruelty, no more greed. . . . But this cannot be seen, only believed and 'understood' by a peculiar gift.*

The people in Merton's Louisville, and the people in the crowd I was watching, were both, in the end, just people. Some were kinder than others, some more successful than others. There were probably some really saintly people there, and probably some really dysfunctional jerks. But mostly, they were just people.

So do I see them as problematic nuisances, annoying, self-absorbed and pushy? Or do I see them walking around shining like the sun?

I think one of the challenges of Catholic Christianity is its tendency to answer either/or questions with both/and answers. Most of us, most of the time, lean toward either/or, because both/and is hard to hold on to.

Christmas is like crowds that way.

On the one hand, Christmas seems to be the one Christian thing that has survived the secularization of society. No matter what your religious beliefs, it sometimes seems, there is an underlying affinity to the winter celebration that highlights the kindness within us and love between us, even if the details are fuzzy or even non-existent about why we're celebrating this good feeling together now. In America, at least, Christmas seems to serve as a generic celebration of goodness. (Even if it's also an excuse for unrestrained avarice and big crowds.)

On the other hand, the secularized version of Christmas, in the interest of inclusion, boils out the whole point of the thing. A Christmas that revolves around Santa and trees and elves, either on shelves or played by Will Ferrell, are not at all a festival to honor the birth of Jesus, who Christians believe was God coming among us as a fellow human.

So is the Mariah Carey version of Christmas an abomination? Or is it just an extension of the true heart of Christmas in a more broadly accessible format?

How you answer that might be a reflection of my crowds dilemma, because they are both an extension of the split between "the world is going to hell in a handbasket" and "love is all around us, if you have eyes to see it." But I think Christmas, perhaps uniquely, underscores that the right answer is both/and.

For those unfamiliar, Christmas is the celebration that God is so crazy-in-love with us humans that He became one of us, to be close to us and help us better recognize that we were made to love God and each other. Merton's revelation at the corner of 4th and Walnut that everyone around him was "shining like the sun" points to the innate loveliness with which we were all created, and which the broader version of Christmas helps celebrate and animate. The fact that God comes not only to be with us, but to help us find our way, points to the glaring need we all have to get out of our self-absorbed (and pushy) way so that we can embrace that better path. Christmas celebrates both that God loves us enough to meet us where we are and that God loves us enough not to leave us there.

Most of us, I suspect, most of the time, lean more on one of those points than the other. In the season of Advent, waiting for Christmas, maybe we have a new opportunity to step outside of the crowd, grab a seat, and reflect on both our tendency to push and shove and the secret beauty of our hearts that sometimes God alone can see.

An Unlikely Christmas Movie

I know that nobody thinks of "Wall Street" as a Christmas movie, but hear me out.

When my now-wife and I were in college, on weekends they would show a late-night movie on campus, as something to do for those who didn't have cars and didn't want to go to frat parties. By the time we graduated, there was a nice movie theater in the student center, but when we were first-year students, the movie was shown in a lecture hall, so no frills. These were dollar movies that were wrapping up their theatrical run. (Given that this was before DVDs were a thing, much less streaming services, I'm teetering over a rabbit hole about what life was like in college in the late 1980s.)

In April of 1988, one of those movies was "Wall Street," the Oliver Stone-directed ode to greed that won Michael Douglas an Oscar (and Darryl Hannah a Razzie, the rare movie with both a best-actor and worst-actress award). It was a December 1987 release, so technically in the Christmas season of what was an incredible year for movies. Listen to this list:

- Planes, Trains and Automobiles
- The Princess Bride
- Lethal Weapon
- Full Metal Jacket
- Predator
- Dirty Dancing
- Robocop
- Fatal Attraction
- The Untouchables
- Moonstruck
- Raising Arizona
- Good Morning Vietnam

- Three Men and a Baby
- No Way Out

I could go on. It was also the year of "Ishtar," "Leonard Part 6," and "Police Academy 4". Truly the best of times and the worst of times.

But "Wall Street" was the movie that was on the screen when I first held this girl's hand, and after which we first kissed. (And, much later, got married.) And so it is one of our favorite movies of all time.

We've gone back to the place where we watched it, and the tree under which we first kissed, and we've even performed in the musical we were working on when we first met, but we've never re-watched "Wall Street" and probably won't. We don't love the movie for anything about the movie. We love the movie because of what it means to us and our story.

I was thinking this year about how Christmas is sort of like what "Wall Street" means to us. We can argue (a lot) about how awful the world is or how wonderful the world is, and the truth is, both arguments have their points. But the Christian claim at Christmas is that God loves *us*, this mess of a creation and this throng of complicated people, so much that God becomes one of us to be *with* us. Not because we're good, nor because we're bad, but because that is the depth of relationship God wants with us. Whether we're good or bad – whether we deserve an Oscar or a Razzie – is irrelevant. Christmas isn't about our performance; it's about what we mean to God and our story together.

If you've ever been in a conversation where everyone is trashing something – a show or a restaurant or a food – and someone is brave enough to say "But I love that," – because it's the show I watched with my parents or the restaurant where my friend works or the dish my grandma used to make – it doesn't just stop the conversation; it changes forever what you think of that thing. You may still think it's awful, but you also know that it means a lot to someone you care about, so you can't quite detest it in the same way you did before. In truth, it's hard not to have some secondhand affection for it.

That's what Christmas is all about, to steal a line. We can't ever be so fed up with each other that we ignore that God chooses us, values us, in a way that we have to honor. Even if we don't quite get what God sees in us. Our value doesn't come from us; it comes from what we mean to God.

And that's what "Wall Street" taught me about Christmas.

(To save you the search, "Die Hard" was released in 1988.)

• • • •

Originally published December 2022

Mattering

What is it that we need, really?

I was at a (secular) conference this week, and one of the speakers, a distinguished 93-year-old "aging rebel," talked about what older people need, using a term born from research that began with juvenile delinquents: Mattering.

We need to feel like we *matter*. Whether we are a child or whether we are an old person, if we think that what we do and who we are matters to someone, we will thrive; if we don't think that, we'll wither.

Mattering is a combination of love and purpose. If I am known and loved by someone I love in return, and if I have a purpose that matters to that loved one, I matter.

This was all very familiar to me. I had a dream a few years ago of pulling together a conference I was going to call "Disrupt Despair." It was going to focus on the fact that the people who study our society's major pathologies – addiction, violence, mass shootings, gang membership, criminality, suicide, extremism – all seemed to point to a lack of healthy connection and purpose – a lack of mattering, as a root cause of their particular pathology. My thought was, if we could identify who might be likely to think they didn't matter – through Adverse Childhood Experience (ACE) scores or online activity or whatever else is knowable – caring people could intervene in ways that communicated to those at risk of despair, "you matter."

That was 2019-2020, and I just couldn't pull it together before the pandemic hit, but I did have the opportunity to talk to enough experts and do enough digging to see that, at least to some degree, the hypothesis was correct. Mattering matters. A lot.

John 4 has a lot of layers, but the main part of the chapter, the story of the Samaritan woman at the well, made me think of mattering, so I'll focus on that here.

For all that is going on in this story, the themes that stick out are about water and food, maybe the two things people would put first on their list of things we all need to live, things at the base of Maslow's hierarchy of needs. Jesus asks the Samaritan woman, alone at the well in the heat of the day, to give him some water, and then in their ensuing discussion reveals that He gives "living water," which satiates every thirst. Then the disciples ask him if he's hungry, and he says he has his own food, because "My food is to do the will of the one who sent me."

Jesus's food is the work that He does. His purpose.

What about the living water?

Let me suggest that what God offers through the story of Jesus, above all, is the message that we matter. All the theological debates about the mysteries of faith are important, I'm sure, but at its essence, the idea that a monotheistic God would create everything and then choose to become one of us, to be with us, is nothing if not a message of mattering.

People are awesome. (Some more than others.) People are limited. (Some more than others.) We can and do matter to each other, and we are better and worse at communicating that effectively.

But the living water that Jesus offers at the well? I'll suggest that it's nothing more and nothing less than that, at the very deepest level of existence, to the one unshakable Lover, we matter.

By the way, the Samaritan woman at the well? Many commentators point out that she was probably there in the heat of the day to get water because she was an outcast (maybe because of her history). She was often used, but not loved. She wasn't acceptable to polite company. She didn't matter.

And if the Disrupt Despair idea has any truth to it, or the mattering research has any validity, that ultimate backstop of mattering to God is indeed living water that can carry us through the heat of any day and give us the reservoir to pursue the food Jesus talks about. So it shouldn't be a surprise that the outcast woman ends up becoming Jesus' most effective evangelist. From being fully known and loved, she did the will of the one who knew and loved her, and did it really well.

So what do we need? We need to matter. And the heart of the Gospel is that we unshakably do.

. . . .

Originally published August 2022

The Difficult Grace of The Passive Voice

My wife is truly a saint in the making, and not only because she puts up with me. She has an unquenchable thirst for God – prioritizing prayer and study. She's great at something I am horrible at – praying for others in her life, not only when they ask for it but just as part of her daily routine. And, as the founder of a moms' prayer group at our daughter's school, she convenes a community of women that she cares deeply for and serves in countless ways. She has organized enough meal drops for sick or recovering members that the "Take Them a Meal" website should consider her for their board, or as a celebrity endorser.

I mention this because, as she recovers from her own health issue, it is readily apparent that she is *very* uncomfortable with the shoe being on the other foot. As her friends rise to the opportunity to reciprocate for all she's done for them, she is grateful, but uneasy. Some of it, I suspect, is the desire not to be the center of attention, but it's more than that. We are trained to think of faith in the active voice – we pray, we worship, we study, and especially we love, by feeding the hungry and caring for the sick and comforting the lonely and sometimes guiding the lost. But if we are all equally children of God, and we live in a community of faith that supports each other, we need to be willing, when needed, to accept the sort of support we freely offer to others.

If you're the type who is used to achieving, used to independence, used to control, being helpless (or at least needing help) is tough. There is inevitable guilt ("think of all the people who are in much worse shape") at being served, when you are used to doing the serving. There is a safety in being the one to offer help; depending on others can feel like the opposite of safety.

But I think it's good for us, to some extent, to accept the difficult grace of the passive voice. When we do, we make evident that there are not two classes of people in God's family – the givers and the receivers

– but that we are all both, all the time. If it is in giving that true joy lies, there is a consideration in letting others embrace that joy at our expense. And the experience of receiving something that you could not attain on your own is to experience the definition of grace and a kind of love that is a reflection of the divine.

I've been reflecting this week on Luke 7, where Jesus goes to a Pharisee's house and a "sinful woman" washes his feet with her tears. There are a lot of dynamics in the story, but one that hadn't struck me before was Jesus' willingness to *let* this woman wash his feet. Late in John's Gospel, when Jesus says he will wash the feet of his disciples, Peter protests – no way, you're the one who should be served. But if we are to be the hands and feet of Christ, that not only means we need to heal and feed and go where Jesus would have us minister; it means we need to let others do the same for us. May we embrace the difficult grace of the passive voice.

• • • •

Originally published January 2016

You Remembered My Name!

"You remembered my name!"

One of the small touches that makes *Ted Lasso* so special is the way lines of dialogue get repurposed throughout the show. The creators of the series do this with bit players, too – a seemingly inconsequential character appears for a moment, recedes completely, and then nine or ten episodes later pops up again in an entirely unexpected scene. The writers do the same thing with lines of dialogue, and it's a nice touch.

In the pilot episode, we meet a character so convinced in his invisibility that, when asked his name, he says "Oh, nobody asks me my name." There's a comically awkward beat before he realizes that, regardless of the fact that nobody else asks him his name, the person who just did still wants to hear it. And the following day, when that person calls him by name, he half-whispers in amazement, "He remembered my name!"

In the second season, about 13 episodes later, a different character, also convinced in her invisibility toward another character, says the same line, with the same emotion: "He remembered my name!" Again, it's a small touch, but it's beautiful to see those points connected. And if you have ever felt invisible, you know the emotion behind the line.

In Luke 16, there is a small detail that is easy to miss at the end of the chapter. Jesus tells the parable of the rich man and Lazarus, and as best as I can tell, this is the only time Jesus gives a character in one of his parables a name. (Confusing things, Lazarus is also the name of the person Jesus raises from the dead in the Gospel of John. The two Lazaruses (Lazari?) are not connected.) This Lazarus is the most outcast, marginalized, powerless, rejected character in any parable Jesus tells; that Jesus gives him a name even as he describes the indignity of his life says something powerful about who God cares about.

The absurdity of Christianity includes the idea that the God who creates and sustains all things cares so deeply and personally about every distinct element of the creation that God knows our names. But the fact that it's only Lazarus that Jesus gives a name to in his storytelling makes a powerful point of its own.

The (nameless) rich man's lack of concern for the poor Lazarus who is dropped at his door brings condemnation on the rich man and his family. Take this parable with the one before it, about a dishonest manager, and the one before that, the prodigal son, and you get a strong theme that Jesus' morality centers deeply on how we use our possessions. In fact, throughout the Gospels, Jesus' moral lessons return again and again to the point that we are to use our stuff to help those who need it – the vulnerable and powerless – rather than waste it selfishly on frivolous things for ourselves.

This isn't just a Jesus thing, of course. Both the Torah and the prophets of the Old Testament underscore the same point: we belong to each other, and we need to use what we have for the benefit of others. This is a clear and consistent point of emphasis throughout Scriptures.

For whatever reason, Christian morality has been primarily connected to having good manners, avoiding bad language, and treating sex chastely. (All things *Ted Lasso*'s characters do not do.) But the more time I spend reading the gospels, the clearer it is that Jesus talked very little about those things, and instead spent his time with sinners and prostitutes, had disciples who flouted good manners, and almost certainly heard a lot of Aramaic cussing. He focused on loving the unlovable and challenged those with power to use it for the benefit of the outcast.

I remain a fan of kindness that shows up in manners, decorum, and chastity, don't get me wrong. But I also realize that if Christians want to live up to the lessons of Scripture, we need to be a little less focused on those things and a lot more on pushing ourselves to use what we have to help those whose names only God bothers to remember.

• • • •

Originally published September 2021

Eulogy for My Father

My father, Paul, passed away in 2015 at the age of 94. Here is what I said at his funeral.

Much to the chagrin of those I work with, I don't follow scripts. But once I figured out what I wanted to say at my dad's service today, I wrote it down.

I am Paul's son, Jeff.

I feel compelled to start with a joke. If you were around my dad at all — if you were a patient in his dentist's chair or a member of his Sunday School class or Sertoma Club or Men's Prayer Breakfast group or bridge or tennis group, you heard a joke. And if you were a member of his family, at his dinner table and in the car on long vacation drives, you heard *all* the jokes.

Some of you know that before Dad was a dentist, he was a Marine pilot in World War II. What I don't think he told anybody but me was that he was once called on for a top-secret mission to fly a special delegation cross-country for an important meeting. He had four passengers: the President of the United States, the country's richest man, the smartest man in the world, and the greatest evangelist of that time.

As sometimes happens in stories like this, Dad's plane had a problem: the fuel line leaked, and they were running out of gas quickly, far from any safe landing spot. Dad put the plane on autopilot (this was a technologically advanced plane for the time) and went back to the cabin and said "Sirs, I regret to inform you that we have two problems. The first is that we are going to crash. The second is that we have only four parachutes for the five of us."

Well, the president reacted quickly, saying "Gentlemen, in this dark time of war our nation needs me more than ever. Were I to perish, the spirit of our country would be shaken and our ability to win this war would be in jeopardy. I must survive." And he took a parachute and jumped out the hatch to safety.

Immediately after, the country's richest man said "Our economy is only now climbing out of the long Depression. Were I to die, the stock market would be shaken, businesses would collapse, and millions would be thrown back into unemployment. I must survive." And he grabbed a parachute and out he went.

Right after that, the world's smartest man said "I have in my mind an idea that will bring peace and prosperity, not only to our country but to the entire world. I must survive to bring that idea to reality." And he followed the other two out the hatch.

The great evangelist looked at Dad and said, "Son, I have lived a good life. I know our Maker and I am not afraid to meet Him. Take the last parachute. I'm ready to die."

And Dad said, "Actually, we still have two parachutes." The evangelist said "It's a miracle! Like the loaves and fishes!"

And Dad said "No, the world's smartest man grabbed my backpack by mistake."

Dad told that joke years ago, but I had forgotten it until my daughter told it to me last summer. So, whether this is comforting or disturbing, know that Dad's humor has been handed down to future generations.

But I tell that particular joke because I see a lot of Dad in its characters.

Dad wasn't the President of the United States. But to be president, you have to deeply love your country, and dad was a great patriot. He really was a Marine pilot in the war, and he really did have a secret mission, which thankfully he never had to execute. While most of the stories I heard of his time in the Pacific were fun and games with his fellow pilots, toward the end of the war they were training for a mission to dive-bomb Tokyo, which would have likely killed thousands and almost certainly cost them their lives. Fortunately for us, their plans were suddenly changed, and they were pulled back from their forward position without explanation. Days later, when the first atomic bomb was dropped on Hiroshima, they understood why their lives had been spared. But long before he met any of us, Dad was prepared to give his life for his country. He continued to serve our nation in the Navy as a dentist, and even after retiring from the military after more than twenty years of service, he remained an active citizen and student of policy and politics. My dad wasn't the President of the United States, but he loved our country.

Dad wasn't the richest man in the country, although he was a great provider for his family. But to be rich you have to know how to invest wisely and take some risks, and Dad did that in what counts. He wasn't rich in money, but he was rich in relationships. He invested his whole heart in his family and friends, and was rich in love for it. And in terms of taking risks... I'm 46, and I'm still two years younger than Dad was when he and Mom adopted me as an infant. I realize more and more what a risk, what an act of optimism that was. Dad wasn't the country's richest man in money, but he invested his heart wisely, and I'm glad he took some risks with it.

Dad wasn't the smartest man in the world, although he was awfully bright. It takes not only a quick wit but a clarity of thought to be truly smart, and Dad had that. My sister mentioned some examples of his wit, but the best example of his clarity of thinking was this: In his early twenties, as the war ended, he realized he needed to decide what to do with his life. So he sat down with a sheet of paper and listed out what he liked to do, what he was good at, and what we wanted out of life, and he decided that being a dentist was the best choice for him. He raced through school, taking chemistry courses out of sequence but acing them anyway, which shows he was smart. But the fact that 60 years after making that decision he was *still* practicing dentistry, because he enjoyed it more than any hobby, is what has always impressed me. People spend thousands of dollars trying to figure out what they want to do with their lives, and some of us never figure it out. Dad just needed a sheet of paper and a sharp pencil. He wasn't the smartest man in the world, but he was a clear thinker.

Dad wasn't the greatest evangelist of his day. To evangelize, you have to preach the good news of Jesus Christ. Dad was a devoted member of this congregation and he and Mom made sure we went to church, and he always prayed at dinner and at family occasions, but other than that, I don't remember him talking about his faith too much. But when I was in Vacation Bible School here as a kid, I remember learning a dippy little song about the fruits of the Holy Spirit, which another Paul, the apostle, listed in Galatians 5:22-23. I have always used these to discern how well I was allowing God to work in my life. I won't sing the song, but listen to the list:

• Love – I've already talked about how richly he loved.

• Joy – My sister already talked about how joyfully Dad lived his life.

• Peace – You know how, when you get to know someone, you can sense if they have some sort of underlying tension in their life that they haven't resolved? Dad had none of that.

• Patience – OK, I can remember Dad getting impatient to get us out the door for things – dinner reservations, vacations, stuff like that. But generally, he was a patient man, especially with four daughters. And in the big things, he was imminently patient with us. He never gave up on any of his relationships, like the father in the Parable of the Prodigal Son, even when some of us strayed off the straight and narrow path, and that's what God's patience looks like. He would get impatient when it was time to go, though, and that was true in his last moments. As he lay dying, he kept saying, "Come on! Let's go! I want to get out of here!" Those of us who were there realized that he wasn't fussing at us to get him out of bed. He was fussing at God to take him home.

• Kindness – We could be here all day swapping stories of his kindness, but one story I tell often. When Dad retired, he and Mom started volunteering as drivers for Meals on Wheels and did that consistently until just a couple years ago. The thought of a 92-year old and his wife taking meals to "the old people" who were often decades younger than them is a testament to their kindness.

• Goodness – I don't know anyone who has ever questioned Dad's good intent.

• Faithfulness – Dad's faithfulness in 67+ years of marriage, in commitment to his family, his friends and his community speaks volumes. His last request was for Mom to be with him.

• Gentleness – Dad was gentle with animals, with children, and with his patients, which is what made him such a beloved dentist. Even in the nursing home where he spent most of the last few months, he frequently thanked and apologized to the staff who were helping him for not being more compliant. That's gentleness.

• Self-control – Whether it was deciding to stop smoking or jogging before jogging was cool, Dad had self-control in abundance. Except when it came to a dish of ice cream.

Francis of Assisi was said to have told his followers "Preach the good news at all times. Use words when necessary." Dad may not have been the greatest evangelist, but he preached the good news with the way he lived his life. He didn't need words.

A central part of that good news is that death does not get the last say and that love wins out. We know that Dad lives in each of us who were changed for the better for knowing him, and we have faith that he lives eternally in God's love. One of the downsides of living to 94 is that many of your friends beat you through heaven's door. So while we know there are many familiar faces in heaven's welcoming party, it's a comfort to our family to have so many friends of his and of ours here today to celebrate his life. Thank you for coming.

• • • •

Originally published March 2015

All y'all, listen a sec.

As is true with the Passion narratives, I have a lot of trouble finding anything that jumps out at me as new or surprising in the infancy narratives of Matthew (or of Luke, really). While there are a lot of great pieces to this opening of the New Testament – all the dreams in Matthew 2, including the impetus of my favorite obscure James Taylor song, "Home By Another Way," for instance – they all feel like well-traveled ground. You've already heard the sermons and homilies.

One thing I did notice in Matthew's third chapter, though, is about John the Baptist's preaching. It's a very slimmed-down version of what you hear in Luke, and it's a lot more focused on threatening the religious elites than it is on challenging the wealthy (which Luke's John the Baptist does). But the Good News translation of Matthew 3:2 has John saying "Turn away from your sins" to the crowd, and I think the translation (which sure sounds like what we always hear) blinds us to stuff that's really important by messing up the singulars and plurals.

It's well known that the English language was vastly improved by American Southerners when they established a real second-person plural: "y'all." (If you think it's "ya'll," I am so sorry.) Unlike virtually every other language, non-southern English lacks a proper demarcation between second-person singulars and plurals, and I think that's problematic here. But so is the pluralizing of "sin" to "sins."

Look, the Greek here is just *metanoia*, which means "change of heart/mind," so we're all riffing a little on the translation. But the Christianity I grew up with really focused on the singularity of the "you" and the plurality of the "sins." And that brought with it an emphasis that faith was about the individual – you "getting right with God" by confessing the specific things you had done wrong.

Which is not a bad thing, as far as it goes. It just doesn't seem to go as far as I used to think.

I could dwell on the limits of this mindset: the OCD legalism that comes with a focus on eliminating specific sins like weeds in a garden; the me-and-God individualism that blithely ignores the social and cultural context in which we live and allows us to personalize faith to the point that we forget that we are all meant by God to be connected to each other, etc.

But let me instead just focus on flipping this around. John the Baptist also means y'all – really, the emphatic "All y'all" – need to repent of your "sin." Actually, he probably means that phrasing first, given how he lights into the religious elites who create the culture there.

When sin is singular, it isn't a to-do list (or, worse, a to-don't list) to check off. It is a state of being. We don't slip and do *sins*. We are existentially mired in *sin*. The first, we can try to work on. The second, we just have to give up, throw our hands up, recognize that we are mired in a culture that is fundamentally messed up, and cry for help.

And when the sin isn't *yours* or *mine* but *ours* (as in an "all y'all"), it doesn't just cover discrete actions by one of us but a system and culture that is the air we breathe together. It is not just about deciding which of us did the worst thing the most times; it is recognizing that we all are in this mess and all need to get each other out of it.

To fix "All y'all turn away from your (collective) sin," we have to recognize that things like consumerism and racism and individualism and sexism and all the other -isms aren't just the libs trying to stick their grievances onto the concept of sin; they are part of the thick muck in which we all live our lives. And unless we, collectively, recognize the muck for what it is and recognize that, no matter how well we dry-clean our own individual dress clothes, the muck still remains, we'll never be open to the change of heart John calls us to at the Jordan.

• • • •

Originally published October 2021

Look for the Lepers

Look, I get the value of Fred Rogers' quote, "Look for the helpers," as a way to soothe children in times of stress by encouraging them to focus on those who are doing good in times of tragedy.

But if you want to find where God is, look to the lepers.

From the time of, say, Moses until the mid-twentieth century, we treated people with Hansen's disease, or leprosy, pretty much the same way. We considered them cursed, vile, evil and degenerate, and we sought to protect ourselves and our loved ones by excluding them from society. For most of human history, having leprosy meant losing all contact with friends and family, facing sanctioned physical abuse, and accepting the responsibility to warn away anyone who would come near you. The disease itself led to a pretty horrible death, but the abandonment and condemnation that preceded the bodily death was worse. If there were worse things than being a leper, I don't know what they were.

In the Old Testament, there are a lot of rules about how to exclude and eliminate lepers from the community, as well as rituals for accepting those who recover from leprosy. But most of the references people know in the Bible about lepers come from the Gospel accounts of Jesus healing them. In some cases, he heals them by telling them to go wash themselves; in others, he actually touches them to heal them. At any rate, he broke all kinds of rules by helping rather than shunning lepers, and for many people, his proximity to lepers would have led to suspicion that he was one of them.

This isn't just a Bible-times thing. A key part of St. Francis of Assisi's story was his metamorphosis from someone who, as part of polite society, despised lepers, to someone who embraced a leper he encountered, to someone who committed himself to living with and caring for those with leprosy.

This isn't just a Medieval thing. When my wife and I went to Hawaii many years ago, the locals were hyped up, because a Hawaiian was about to be named a saint by the Catholic Church. St. Damien of Molokai was a 19th century Belgian missionary who was sent to Hawaii and took on a ministry to the leper colony of Molokai, moving to the place where the shunned were sent and turning it into a community, until he succumbed to the disease himself.

The throughline here is not the disease; it's that God and the godly go where people are shunned and excluded and live with the people that everyone else would rather not see.

This is still a thing today. For the most part, it isn't Hansen's disease that leads to people being shunned and excluded. But a lot of us treat other people struggling with other challenges the same way – by kicking them out, by hunting them down, by proclaiming they aren't worthy of basic dignity.

We should probably remember that, if we don't embrace the lepers, if we don't put in the center those who everyone else excludes, we aren't following the example of Damien. Or Francis. Or Jesus.

If you want to find God in the world, look for the lepers, and go stand with them.

Who are the heroes, and who are the villains?

Who are the seekers, and who are the sought?

What does peace require?

Entering the home stretch of Luke – literally, as Jesus enters Jerusalem and cleans up the temple in Luke 19 – there are some big questions to answer.

Heroes and villains – if you are like me, the story of Zaccheus, the little tax guy who climbs a tree to see Jesus, is one you have known since you were a kid. In fact, if you were a Vacation Bible School kid, you may be hearing a song in your head even now, "Zaccheus was a wee little man, a wee little man was he ..." If so, I'm sorry.

I never realized that Zaccheus was the last encounter Luke chronicles before Jesus enters Jerusalem. I also didn't connect that in the chapter before, Luke encounters the (unnamed) "rich young ruler." In fact, Luke uses the same word (the Greek one for "rich") to describe both the guy in Luke 18 and Zaccheus.

That guy, the unnamed rich guy, was a hero. He was rich, popular, probably good-looking even, and he could go toe-to-toe with Jesus in citing the law. The stuff Jesus asked him to do, the commandments? That guy said "check, check, check."

Zaccheus was a villain, for sure. I mean, he was a *tax guy!* Not just a run-of-the-mill auditor (like Matthew), either; he ran the regional office. Collecting taxes for a pagan empire was (and for many still is) villainous business. Zaccheus may have been rich, but nobody was going to lift a finger to help him see Jesus. He was bad news.

Except when Jesus asked the unnamed guy to give up his possessions and join him, he walked away. And we know that he was seen as a hero, because when he walked away, the disciples all said, "Well, shoot, if *that* guy can't get into heaven, how do *we* have a chance?"

And except when Jesus told Zaccheus "I'm coming to your place for dinner," Zaccheus made a statement that my former (unrelated) teacher Luke Johnson pointed out: Zaccheus didn't suddenly have a change of heart (like I always thought) and announce what he was *gonna* do; instead, what he told Jesus was, "Hey, just so you know, I give half my possessions to the poor and pay back anyone who got scammed by me or my people four times over." This isn't Ebenezer Scrooge, and Jesus isn't the Ghost of Christmas Future. Zaccheus was just a guy who had been pegged as a heel but kept taking care of those who were more outcast than he was, even if nobody noticed.

Who seeks whom? – Luke uses the same verb at the beginning and the end of the story. Zaccheus was seeking Jesus, but in the end, Jesus says he was coming to "seek and save the lost." In my limited experience, this is exactly how it works. We may think that we need to go find God, but we're being silly. Especially if we feel like we have a ton of baggage that God won't accept, we're going to be surprised to find out, eventually, that it's God who has been seeking *us*, not to straighten us up but to wrap us up in mercy and acceptance.

"If you only knew what it takes to have peace!"

Jesus says that (a loose translation) in Luke 19:42, about Jerusalem, on the approach to the big entry into town we mark at Palm Sunday. And I've been thinking a little bit about what peace requires.

We live in a time of retributive justice. Later in this book, you'll hear about my former colleague who liked to bellow "You're off the list!" when someone crossed him. It is definitely the ethic of the day, both among Christians and in the world at large. When people sneer about "cancel culture," this is the grain of truth they are surfacing; the fact that, if someone does wrong, many of us judge them as irredeemable. At its best, this response comes from a place of seeking peace through retribution.

Whether we are talking about personal relationships, or political fights, or legal battles, or military actions, surely we have figured out by now that retribution is not what it takes to have peace. You can keep doing that stuff until we are all eye-less and tooth-less, and it will not bring the peace you need in your gut; it just sets up the next fight.

Jesus doesn't say what it is, exactly, that Jerusalem didn't realize it needed to have peace. The gospel writers make the obvious answer to that question Jesus. But if we really buy into that – if we let peace in like Zaccheus let Jesus come to dinner, instead of walking away like the rich guy who didn't want to share his stuff – maybe we have to realize that retributive justice is never going to work, and we start to work toward restorative justice. And – this is the hard part – we begin to realize that none of us are heroes or villains, just lost folks being sought.

● ● ● ●

Originally published September 2021

Wrong Summit?

Apparently mountaineers encounter this challenge of false summits. (I heard this in a homily by Father Mike Schmitz.) They think they're climbing to the summit of a mountain, and when they break through the clouds to get to the top of where they are climbing, they realize that it's not really the highest point. The next thing over is taller. (Sometimes, apparently, this can happen repeatedly, where each peak yields to an even higher one. As someone whose only mountain adventures are Space, Thunder and, until its demise, Splash, I think mountaineers are nuts to fall for that trick more than once.)

What if Christians picked the wrong thing to make their central sacrament? What if we have the wrong summit?

The Catholic Church in the U.S. recently launched a multiyear campaign to re-emphasize the Eucharist as the "source and summit" of our faith, which I am almost all for. The impetus for this was a Pew survey that showed that only a minority of Catholics actually believe that the Eucharist is what the Church says it is (the Real Presence of Jesus Christ in the consecrated bread and wine). I suspect my political friends will see some potential pitfalls in investing millions of dollars in a campaign to respond to one poll, but let's set that aside for now. Regardless of what Pew says, it's pretty clear that a bunch of people who are either modestly active or fallen-away Catholics don't seem super motivated by the opportunity to commune with God in the Eucharist, so I can see why the bishops would want to change that.

As the global Church goes through its own multiyear journey of listening for the Holy Spirit, I was ready to argue that highlighting the faith we have in common (like in the Eucharist), might help us contextualize and understand the relatively unimportant nature of our differences as we yearn for unity. (Even if most of the popular discussion of the Eucharist is around who particular bishops are threatening to withhold it from.)

But John 13 throws a curveball. Because the core action in Jesus' Last Supper with the disciples is not the institution of the Eucharist. It's something else.

On Holy Thursday, the Thursday of Easter Week, Catholics around the world (and some other folks) celebrate what Jesus does in John 13. The priest (or priests) wash the feet of some representative parishioners. (Except for Pope Francis, who goes to wash the feet of people like Muslim prisoners, to push the point of who God loves beyond the front pews.) It's awkward, and I think most people are happy not to be the ones who have to have their feet washed, and generally we get through it and get back to normal Catholic stuff as quickly as we can. Like the Eucharist.

But what if that foot washing were the daily-repeated main event, instead of the supper?

After Jesus washes the disciples' feet in John 13 (including Judas, I might add), he tells them that the main thing he wants for them to do is love one another. And whatever the foot-washing means, it is a humbling sign of loving care for each other.

If we're worried that people aren't as excited about being Catholic, or Christian, as they used to be, maybe we should ask whether we picked the wrong example from Jesus' life to make into a daily exercise. If a community committed itself each week, and maybe even each day, to commemorating God's guidance to love each other by washing each other's feet, would it have the same problems convincing people that it was worth joining and sticking with? It probably wouldn't struggle to convince people that they cared about each other, and people might not fight to be at the top of a power pyramid if that meant, primarily, washing everyone else's smelly size 12s.

Would making that practice our apex of communal worship be a higher summit? I don't know. I'm glad we celebrate the Eucharist more than once a year because I need all the supernatural help I can get. But

I bet the Church would look different if we focused more on washing each others' feet than about who gets to eat at the table.

• • • •

Originally published December 2022

Because Facebook knows marketing, I have ads for Catholic T-shirts. (Go figure.) The first one to pop up was of St. Catherine of Siena, with the caption: "Be you. Set the world on fire."

She is one of my top-5 favorite saints, but what I loved about that ad is that it showed up the day that my daughter confessed that she'd love to design fireworks shows someday. I don't think that's what Catherine meant, but you do you, as they say.

If I'm being honest, I'm still sorting out what exactly "you do you" looks like for me. Because it seems like, a lot of times, "you do you" means finding your way on a path that doesn't fit into the culture's binary choices.

Jesus does this a lot. I think about the time that he came upon a woman caught in adultery (John 8). The gang of leaders wanted Jesus to endorse them killing her, and presumably the other option would have been to fight off the mob on her behalf. But instead he wrote in the dirt, threw out a prerequisite that they weren't prepared for ("Let the one without sin throw the first stone"), and waited for the crowd to melt away. An unimagined third response.

Or when they asked Jesus whether or not to pay taxes (Matthew 22). The binary options were "yes – submit to the foreign empire" and "no – fight the power," and instead he asks whose face is on the coins and then says, pay that guy his due, but pay God *his* due as well. An unimagined third response.

St. Francis of Assisi (who didn't actually say "Preach the gospel at all times. Use shirts when necessary." even if it *is* a good T-shirt) sort of modeled this, too. He lived during the Crusades – he actually set off to fight in one before his conversion – and the option was really to fight against the Islamic rulers who occupied the Holy Land or acquiesce and, well, mind your own business. Francis didn't do either of those. He took a brother with him to meet the sultan and try to make peace (by converting the sultan to Christianity). That Francis wasn't martyred was a surprise, even to him, but it showed the power of an unimagined third response, and is why it's Franciscans who still run the Christian devotional sites in the Holy Land.

In the gospels, Jesus said both "if you're not with us, you're against us" (Matthew 12:30) and "if you're not against us, you're with us" (Mark 9:40, Luke 9:50), but this world definitely leans heavily on the side of the former. I get declared somebody's enemy for not being sufficiently committed to their side a dozen times before lunch, in a dizzying variety of settings. (I'm pretty sure you do, too.) The issues people are fighting over are at turns momentous and eye-rolling, but regardless, the choice is always "Are you in, or are you out?" No third option.

I am still looking for some unimagined third responses. The examples that inspire me are self-effacing, even to the point of self-sacrifice. They are humble and yet bold. And they shift the focus in ways that unsettle the parties at war, focusing not on the battle line, but on some question or perspective that helps shake the confident and recast the enemies according to their common humanity.

We need the grace to imagine more unimagined third responses – at least I do. Because in enough areas of my life, I yearn to show up in a way that resets the conflict, even if it's in a way that's weird enough that people shake their heads and say "You do you."

It's the openness to imagine, and courage to enact, those kinds of responses to our intractable conflicts that would truly set the world on fire, like an inspiring fireworks show rather than a dangerous arson.

So you do you, and set the world ablaze.

Too Little, Too Late?

Who decides what is too little, too late?

I was on a conference call today where someone said one of the more honest things I've heard lately on a call like this. She prefaced a question with "I'm sorry, I was multitasking, so I didn't catch what you said…" That is as close to "I wasn't paying attention to you but just realized that you might (surprisingly) have said something important," as you will likely get on one of those calls. Much respect to the person who 'fessed up on that.

I tend to think that most of the gospels come together in that frame of mind, so it doesn't bug me much when they don't get the details quite the same. My theory (which I learned from actual experts) is that the experience of the resurrected Jesus was the thing that made Christianity, and so it was only at that point, after the earthly life of Jesus, that his followers realized that they probably should have paid more attention to the details. If, in reconstructing the facts later, the gospel writers fill in minutiae in their stories that differ from the other accounts, well, that's what happens when you don't pay proper attention the first time. They didn't know this was going to be on the test.

John works from different traditions and in a different style than the other gospel writers, and it shows. One example that I hadn't realized before comes right after the death of Jesus. They all, interestingly, mention that a guy named Joseph of Arimathea provides the tomb in which Jesus is buried. (Fun fact: nobody *really* knows where Arimathea was.) And they all agree that the time was getting late so everyone was in a rush to get Jesus buried before the sabbath started. But in Mark and Luke, women come back after the sabbath to prepare the body, and that's why they're in the vicinity to discover the resurrection.

John's version is different. Joseph of Arimathea is joined by Nicodemus in preparing the body right then for burial. (As in Matthew, there's not really an explanation for why Mary Magdalene was going to the tomb on Easter morning.)

This might be just one of those missed details in the reconstruction of the story, but I'm not so sure. Since Mary Magdalene was the first to discover that Jesus was risen, the details of why she was out there at the tomb are awfully germane, and kick in right when everyone would have quit multitasking and started paying attention. If she was out there to prepare the body, that detail would have been there from the beginning (as it is in Mark, the oldest of the gospels).

So why did John go another way? Why bring back Nicodemus and pair him with Joseph of Arimathea?

Both of these two were insiders, members of the religious elite with reputations to uphold. All the gospels talk about Joseph being a secret disciple, and John has Nicodemus appear three times: first at night, so as not to be found talking with Jesus, then putting up a half-hearted fuss at Jesus' trial about due process, and then here, at the burial.

Both were low-investment disciples who would not risk their positions to profess their belief in the upstart from Galilee. There were probably others who melted away in the night and never came back. The two leaving Jerusalem on the road to Emmaus in Luke are similarly opting out, but Nicodemus and Joseph, at least in theory, were in the room where Jesus' execution was decided, and they didn't stop it. Too little, too late.

Except, by stepping forward to take the body, they had to finally admit to Pilate and to their buddies that they were on Jesus' side. After the seeming fact, when Jesus was already dead, they gave up their status in favor of their beliefs. We don't have a lot of history of what happened to them next, but the assumption is that they were ostracized and kicked out of the Sanhedrin and the synagogue. The only place they would have had to turn was the community of disciples that they studiously avoided associating with when Jesus was alive.

In both the Orthodox and Catholic traditions, Nicodemus and Joseph of Arimathea are venerated as saints. Apparently, showing up after the execution to help bury the corpse with decorum wasn't seen as too little or too late to the Church. And some theorize that John tells their story with an eye toward the people in his own time who believed secretly and timidly from inside the power structure.

Today? Same. When Jesus points to the hungry and thirsty and stranger and exposed and sick and imprisoned in Matthew 25 and says "everyone of those is actually me you're either caring for or ignoring," it's really easy for me to count the times I've turtled in rather than reached out to those folks. When you see that the people Jesus prioritized with his time and attention were the undesirables, the outcasts, the foreigners and the scapegoats, well, there are more of those around today than I could get to even if I tried. Which I have not, honestly.

But tomorrow is another day. And in the meantime, I can root for Nicodemus and Joseph of Arimathea, hoping that it's still not too late to quit multitasking and pay attention to the assignment.

There's a lot of power in shredding your past.

As a convert to Catholicism, I was not initially a big fan of the sacrament of reconciliation (or confession, as it's generally known). I was a firm believer that you didn't have to confess your sins to another person, since you could always confess them directly to God. Even though I never actually did.

I'm still pretty awkward at the whole thing. Mostly, it's because I wasn't raised on the rote prayers Catholics learn early on – I stumble through the "Bless us, O Lord" dinner blessing that every Catholic kid can spit out in 10 seconds or less if they're hungry – so I get a little tangled in the process of the rite. I like to think that it keeps things fresh for the priest to have someone make up their own act of contrition, but what do I know.

I have to tell you, though, if you make yourself do it, reconciliation is a profoundly freeing experience. And I have learned that, for me, the best part isn't when the priest pronounces the absolution of my sins or I do my penance (which, if we're being honest, is usually ridiculously easy).

It's when I rip up the paper.

See, I have had the experience of going to reconciliation, coming out of the booth, and realizing I forgot something I wanted to get clean with God on. (Then I usually curse, which I guess doubles my list for the next time immediately.) So I have gotten in the habit, in preparing for reconciliation, of writing down the things that I know have kept me from being what I should be, so I don't forget when I'm in the booth.

When I leave, having covered all the things on the list, I tear up the paper into tiny pieces and throw it away (usually at the bottom of the kitchen trash when I get home). It's partly a records-retention strategy, but really, it's a tangible sign to myself that those particular things are no longer valid. They are no longer things to feel guilty about. If they ever really held me back from being my best self, they are no longer. The slate is clean.

That is an incredibly powerful, freeing experience. And, so as not to spoil any recent cinematic examples of someone carrying something around for a long time and then tearing it up when it had lost its power, I'll refer you to my favorite movie, *The Mission*.

If you haven't seen the gorgeously shot, angelically scored 1986 classic starring Jeremy Irons and Robert DeNiro, well, that's on you. Go take care of that right now. (I just found out it's on YouTube; I'll be blocking off 2 hours and 6 minutes very soon to rewatch).

For those who saw it back in the day, you will recall that DeNiro was a slaver who came to faith and joined Irons and his band of Jesuits as they ministered to the very same indigenous tribes that DeNiro had once preyed on. For his penance, DeNiro chose to climb the ridiculously treacherous mountainside to the tribe's cliffside home while dragging the heavy weight of his former tools of aggression behind him. At one point, Irons, so frustrated by how impossible a burden DeNiro had chosen for himself, cuts the cord, sending the armor clattering down the mountain. And DeNiro pushes Irons roughly aside, goes down to get it, and starts his arduous climb again.

I mean, sure, ripping up a piece of scratch paper is a lot easier. But the principle is the same: when DeNiro finally lays down his burden of his own choice, he is truly free. (And, being the actor that he is, you will know it.)

(By the way, if you only think of Jeremy Irons as Scar from *Lion King*, add that to your scrap of paper, because it's a sin to ignore how good an actor he is.)

John 21 is almost certainly a late addition to the text, and the story – Jesus encounters some of the disciples while they're fishing – is iconic, deeply symbolic, and leaves me with questions. (Why is Nathanael in this scene, but not Peter's brother Andrew? And Peter fishes naked? That seems unsafe.) But the scene around the fire, where

Jesus asks Peter "Do you love me?" three times in order to unwind the three times Peter denies Jesus in the Passion — that's the shredding of the paper that Peter needs to become the rock you could build on.

I guess here's the point. I spend a lot of time with recurring thoughts running around my head, and usually they won't let me sleep until I write them down, at which point they lay off for a while. If they're "to-dos," which usually they are, they stay in the background until I cross them out, which is almost as good as ripping them up. But if they're a really big deal, I'll tear up the to-do list, or the thing I screwed up, or the thing I'm holding against someone, whether I have the chance to tell them or not. And I am always more free when I do that.

So, if you've wronged someone you can't apologize to directly, or if you're beating yourself up over something you let yourself down on, let me suggest you write it down. Then speak it to whoever you need to speak it to, present or not. Then tear up the paper and let it all go.

In John's telling, it was an unwinding like that which freed Peter to be Peter. Who knows what it will free you to be?

The Most Jesus-y Thing My Church Does

Our church held its annual festival last weekend. Now, I grew up in a respectable Southern Protestant household, so this was foreign to my childhood. If we wanted to ride marginally safe spinny rides, our only outlet was the county fair.

On its face, the festival is a pure sellout to the devil, raising money for the church school by selling cheap thrills, bingo and fried foods galore. It attracts all sorts of people, including several who I'm sure have never darkened the door of a church except to sneak into the bathroom. To make it worse, it happens during Lent, when we're supposed to be solemnly fasting, abstaining and atoning.

But our pastor of the past 20 or so years is a wise man, and while most people who are aware of the festival (and it draws from across the area) think it's timed to be close to St. Patrick's Day, not so, he insists. It's timed each year to fall on the weekend of *Laetare Sunday,* which marks a sort of "halftime break" for Lent. While Sundays remain a feast day, even in Lent, the readings for this week are particularly joyful, reminding us that Lenten fasting is only for a season. This year, the Gospel was the Parable of the Prodigal Son (or the story of the Prodigal Father, which may be a more accurate name). And while listening to that Gospel for the millionth time, I realized that the festival was perhaps the most "Jesus-y" thing our parish does.

I don't mean for a moment that our faith community doesn't show lots of other glimpses of the body of Christ. We worship. We partner with the poor and oppressed, through our sister-parish relationship with a church in Haiti. We try to live out the challenge of Matthew 25 by feeding the hungry through local outreach efforts like St. Vincent DePaul. We learn together to grow in discipleship.

But at the beginning of the reading, before you get into the parable, you learn that what prompted Jesus' telling of it was the grumbling of the Pharisees and scribes that Jesus "welcomes sinners and tax

"

collectors and eats with them." And when the parable itself turns from the prodigal son come home to the do-good son who stayed behind, it says that what sets the "good son" off is "the sound of music and dancing" from the homecoming celebration.

Since we've been doing it so long, I suspect most people who might be offended by the lack of Lenten decorum in our festival have either made their peace or moved to another, more respectable parish. I'm sure there are still a few who grumble about the noise, the mess, or the parking.

The rules of good Christian decorum would say that, if you want to come back to Mother Church, you should show up on Ash Wednesday, do some serious penance, maybe take a class or two, and when you're "ready," come back for good. And if you're just trying to be respectable, at least make it to the dress-up services at Christmas and Easter.

Yet as surely as the love of the prodigal father short-circuits the reinstatement plan of the prodigal son and skips straight from indentured servitude to the full homecoming of a lost son, so, I would argue, does our festival offer everyone the opportunity to celebrate a homecoming to our community, just as Jesus did when celebrating with sinners and tax collectors.

During the weekend, I sat next to a couple (playing bingo) who said they weren't members of the church "anymore," but they still come back to festival each year because it's fun and homey and reminds them of their connection to the place. I ran into another old friend who said she had fallen out of the habit of Church, once her kids had flown the nest, but she realized that it was important, and festival was her first step back. Is festival "enough" to be a part of God's family? Common sense would say, no, you need to show up for Mass and throw something in the offering plate. But who are we to say?

Whether it's the Pharisees of Jesus' day or the "good Christians" of today, it seems to be an easy slip to let our zeal for righteousness translate into a "Gospel for the good enough," a way of acting that implies (if not overtly states) that you have to meet some minimum standards to fall within the circle of God's love. The music and the dancing and the celebration of homecoming reminds us that the Gospel isn't for the good enough; it's for all of us. Whether you come home to festival to reconnect with family or friends, to ride rides, eat fried foods or dance to loud music, it all happens within the benevolent shadow of our church because we know that that's our ultimate family, our ultimate home, and even when we're "supposed to" be serious, our Prodigal Father is always ready to deep-fry the fatted calf and cue the band. That's what the father said to the older, "do-good" son. That's what Jesus said to the scribes and Pharisees who "tut-tutted" him. That's what our Church reminds all of us in its most Jesus-y moment.

• • • •

Originally published March 2016

We were made for joy.

If you watch children at all, you know that. Laughter, skipping, a silly verve for life are such a part of childhood that even in war-torn countries and refugee camps you can find children playing.

Of course, we drive it out of them as soon as we can. In school, joy can be disruptive, so we wall it off to the courtyard of play-time, which gets curtailed as soon as we can fill their days with scheduled after-school activities and homework, where coaches and teachers further underscore that the point is to get serious and settle down.

We do this, basically, to get people ready for adulthood, where joy is not really a public phenomenon. In the past week, I surreptitiously polled two groups – one in person, and one on Facebook – about what gives them joy. Family (including furry family and families of choice), hobbies, and nature were almost all of the responses. A few people (less than 5) talked about the impact of their (usually volunteer) work. Again, joy is a private, rather than a public phenomenon. But everyone who responded should count themselves lucky – at least they had an answer top of mind.

In the last couple of years we have begun talking about "flow," which is sort of like joy, except you can't smile and it has to be in service to your employer.

All of this is wrong.

. . . .

I'll posit a definition for joy, which is one of those things that can be tough to define but you know when you see it. Let's try this: Joy is the feeling you get when you are doing what you feel like you were meant to do, with the people you were meant be with, in the place you were meant to be. Joy is the feeling of the soul at play. Joy is both in the journey and the destination; there is a satisfaction from accomplishment that sparks joy, but there is a joy in the process in knowing you are doing your part to its fullest to get there. Joy is infectious, as is its opposite, which I'll label malaise. And you can choose to be open to joy; you can do the same activity with or without joy (and people can tell the difference from 50 feet away).

As I just defined it, you might think that joy needs to be reserved for something *important*. I think that misunderstands what I mean by "what we are meant for." In his many books and talks, Matthew Kelly talks often about "becoming the best possible version of yourself." That happens at a lot of different levels of what we would usually think of as "important" and acknowledges that we each have different roles to play in different arenas of our lives. Kids are meant to play. So are adults – and not just at home or at the beach, but everywhere.

The one thing I remember about the movie *Chariots of Fire* besides the slow-motion running to music was a quote by the Scottish missionary and Olympic runner Eric Liddell. When he was asked in the film how someone with such a serious, important role could spend his time on something as trivial as running, his response was "I believe God made me for a purpose, but he also made me fast. *When I run, I feel God's pleasure.*" While God did not make *me* fast, there are times when I swim that I feel God's pleasure. That's what joy is.

I have seen joy in unlikely people and places. Not long ago, when the city pool where I swim was undergoing renovation of its locker rooms, the city had port-a-potties installed, and I remember several mornings leaving the pool as the guy whose job it was to service the port-a-potties was about his work. And he was joyous, in how he greeted people and how he acted. Cleaning port-a-potties before dawn. One of the people who runs the front desk at that pool is far happier than anyone should be expected to be at that early hour, anywhere, much less working a front desk. "Peace and love," she shouts with a smile to you as you leave. They choose the joy they were made for.

· · · ·

About 20 years ago, I was working at a small university in Mississippi as the sports information director and *de facto* public affairs officer for the school. One of the things I did was send a weekly email to everyone on campus about what sporting events were coming up. I remember one time, after seeing the school's theater group put on a show, I put this reflection into my weekly email (paraphrased; my record-keeping is worse than my memory):

There are lots of reasons to go to a sporting event or to a live musical performance, and there are lots of reasons not to. Go to one this week though, for this reason. What I saw at the show last week that grabbed my attention more than the songs themselves was the look on the faces of the performers. They said, not with their words but with the way they performed, that they had done everything they could to prepare for their role, they knew they had the talent to do it well, and they knew they were at the top of their game.

I recognized that look, because I see it in our athletes in the midst of competition. That look of joy is one you only really see in theater and sports. But it does us good to get to witness it. Maybe it will rub off, even.

· · · ·

What faith brings to this discussion is this: We make the claim that the highest joy you can feel, the best-possible-best-possible-version-of-yourself, is in fulfilling the role God has in mind for you to love Him and the people he puts in your path as much as you possibly can, and use what gifts you've been given to their fullest. What we say we believe is that there are lots of other ways to be joyful, and they are wonderful, but they exist to give us a hint of a more perfect joy that comes from soaking in the love of the divine Lover.

We say that we believe that. It's pretty rare that we live that way, though. Instead, we spend a lot of time talking down the lesser joys, pooh-poohing and tsk-tsking silliness rather than offering an even more joyful presence to the world.

It would be great, if instead, we worked on choosing the joy before us and striving for the joy we were made for.

C astle, caravan, or cookout?

Some people see the church, and the country, as a castle. A fortress with fortifications constructed to protect the good from the evil. The good people from the evil people. The good values, society, norms and history from the decadent. The truth from lies. The pure from spoil. Usually, it seems, the castle protects the past from the future. Whether in the religious or political expression, it is fundamentally conservative in the truest sense of the term.

Other people see the church, and the country, as a caravan. A community of people on a journey, traveling together, growing together, pilgrims on the way to the future. The caravan grows as it goes, as new pilgrims join the trek. The individual pilgrims become something better than they were before through the experience of community and the lessons learned and boundaries stretched along the way. We may never reach the Promised Land in this lifetime, but we can get closer if we are willing to venture forth. Usually, it seems, the caravan focuses on finding a future that is better than the past. Whether in the religious or political expression, it is fundamentally progressive in the truest sense of the term.

This dichotomy seems to be at the root of a lot of our divisions today, and I think it reflects, to some degree, two different personalities shaped by two different cultures. Most personality inventories have some version of this dualism; the language that sticks with me is "need for certainty" vs. "tolerance for ambiguity." Others substitute "growth mindset" for that latter term, I think.

You probably have picked a side in this battle; frankly, it's hard not to these days.

But the more these two worldviews wrestle for supremacy, the more I think they both risk missing the point.

The church, and the country, could be a cookout. Cookouts are rooted in the present. They don't generally have an agenda, or an initiation rite. They are not "about" anything, really, other than the opportunity to celebrate together, with minimal structure or even dress code, our proximity, our neighborliness, our love. You show up, you bring what you can bring, you enjoy what others have brought, you have fun.

If that sounds impossibly unserious, reflect that it may be at least as Biblically rooted. The pre-eminent message of the New Testament: Love. The thing Jesus wishes for people: Peace. The thing the angels call us to do: Rejoice. The most scandalous thing Jesus does, consistently, throughout the Gospels? Carouse with impolite company.

Sounds like a great cookout to me. May we never get so caught up in arguing about what we need a castle to protect or what we need to caravan together to go discover that we forget to fire up the grill and celebrate the open space we share right now.

• • • •

Originally published January 2022

What do you do with an abandoned temple?

The city where I live is going through one of its periodic building booms, and one thing I've noticed about living in a place that lacks undeveloped land is that there has been a huge wave of "tear-downs." Builders will purchase a lot and whatever is on it — whether it's a relatively new and certainly habitable house or an old gas station or motel — and tear down what was there so they can start fresh with a monstrous new construction. (I guess to make the financial math work, you have to be willing to build something big.) A lot of what we've lost, I haven't missed. In fact, frequently I'll see a newly vacant lot and spend the next half-hour trying to remember what was there before.

Sometimes, the local neighborhood or the historic preservation society will put its collective foot down in the face of this slow march of bulldozers and claim that a structure needs to be saved. They don't always win (in truth, they don't often win), but when they do, a developer has the challenge to turn a building that was meant for another purpose into something they can sell now. You get some really interesting concepts out of that — banks turned into steakhouses with the vault becoming a private dining room, for instance. These reimaginings don't always work, but they're at least creative.

And sometimes, it's a lot simpler than all that. Restaurants become new restaurants, with only the signage changing. When I was a kid, Pizza Huts had a very distinctive architecture, with a particular slope of roof. We have restaurants that are not Pizza Huts living in those buildings now. The purpose didn't change, just the menu and the logo.

So it is with places of worship. Not far from me are six big houses where there once was an old church, most recently the Open Bible Church, that changed names frequently but apparently did not find a sustainable congregation. Down the street from me, the former Church of the Beatitudes was bought, deconsecrated (to the extent that American Baptists do that kind of thing), and turned into a very unique home. (They also built three other McMansions on the former parking lot and parsonage.)

But my favorite is in the Piazza del Comune of Assisi, Italy, where sits the church of Santa Maria Sopra Minerva. (St. Mary on top of Minerva). As the traditional Roman columns make clear, the good folks of Assisi, after adopting Christianity, took the local temple devoted to the Roman goddess Minerva and just added Jesus on top of it, reconsecrating it into a church devoted to Mary.

This threefold model applies to figurative abandoned temples, too. Some of the things I have made into idols, I have to just get rid of, because there's no way to reconcile them to a God-first life. Some, I can recycle, putting them into a new place in my life's hierarchy, where they fill a role that isn't idolatrous. And some parts of my life have an essential holiness that just needs Jesus added on top.

The challenge is knowing which is which. You'll see in my thoughts below that in many cases, I am still sorting that out. I have a suspicion that I always will, in part because as my relationship with God evolves and I (hopefully) grow, the way I look at other things will change, too.

. . . .

What keeps me from recognizing the worth of every human life?

That's one question that surfaces where the idols have been in my life. Another is:

What would I choose over God?

My reaction to my three weeks of political ping-pong, I now realize, was part of a growing conviction that the world we have built for ourselves — the political and economic systems, the culture of celebrity — is just incompatible with the idea that every human life is of inestimable worth. It is harder and harder for me not to see that in the things we put at the center of importance in our world.

But I have far more powerful idols I have still had to wrestle with. And the reality is that the attractions of political and national tribalism, of celebrity and ambition, of consumerism and hedonism — of all the things that our society holds up as more important than God and reasons to forget the inestimable value of every life — have roots in some foundational idols that these societal forces seed and feed.

One is purpose — or more pointedly, the belief that I have more value than others to God because (or if) I have a special purpose that is extra-cool.

Another is pride — which is a broader belief that I'm just a little more worthy than everyone else, either because of the tribes I belong to or the things I take credit for.

A third is control — which, if I'm honest with myself, is the belief that I know better than God how to live my life.

A fourth is relationships — both the ones I would put ahead of God in my pecking order of priorities and those that carry with them a hidden belief that I am worth more than those I relate to.

Maybe the hardest one, though, is distraction. I think it was Corrie ten Boom who said "If the devil can't make you bad, he'll make you busy." Maybe that's true, I don't know. But I do know that valuing God first, and valuing every life inestimably, is swimming hard against the currents of culture, which makes it easy to get distracted. Even though I may in the abstract recognize the inestimable value of every life, it's easy for me to forget that, in the face of distractions big and small.

As with the reflections above, many of these were written long before these realizations. I've included these as a trail of breadcrumbs on my convoluted journey toward recognizing my idols, abandoning their temples, and letting God raze, repurpose, or rededicate them.

Purpose

Augustine was right, of course.

Sort of out of the blue, I was reminded that about 4 to 5 years ago, I started looking into the research on the root causes of a range of social maladies that we tend to group under the heading of despair: suicide, addiction, gun violence, gang membership, violent extremism. When you look at what the experts list as the most likely factors that lead people down these various paths, the lists look pretty similar. Though measured and expressed in different ways, two major factors that seem most likely to predict despair loom large: lack of purpose and lack of belonging.

Through those twin lenses, you can see how membership in antisocial groups like gangs or extremist groups address in a stunted way the lack of belonging, and those two (plus in many cases, gun violence) create grotesque versions of purpose. So I concluded back then that the way for a society to get ahead of these dysfunctions was to create pathways for the lost and excluded to find prosocial sources of belonging and opportunities that bring a healthy sense of purpose.

But what, really, is a healthy sense of purpose? We can agree that the categories of despair are the opposite of healthy, but how healthy are more socially acceptable purposes?

In a separate conversation, I was talking with someone who was heading toward retirement and was clearly and vocally uncomfortable with the idea that they would not be getting a paycheck. In this person's case, the issue wasn't financial need; it was a recognition that, for them, purpose was tied to a job that they got paid for.

That's obviously far superior as purposes go to gang loyalty. But I'm not sure how healthy it is. I know many people who have found themselves unable to leave work behind, and frankly unable to even sit still, because, for them, purpose is defined by busy-ness. Those folks will potentially get a lot of things done for themselves and others that could well be good. But perpetual busyness comes with costs, from physical, mental and emotional exhaustion to stresses on relationships to a lack of time for reflection, rest, and renewal. Even if being productive is the most popular purpose in American society, I'm not at all convinced that it's a sufficiently healthy one.

Way back in the 4th century, St. Augustine of Hippo wrote what is considered by many to be the first spiritual autobiography, his *Confessions*. The opening lines of the book are a prayer: *You have made us for yourself, O Lord, and our heart is restless until it rests in you.*

We are made for God, which is to say, we are made for Love, and our heart is restless until we come to understand that.

You can be busy for love, but you can also be still for love. And you can definitely be busy (or still) for reasons other than love.

If we really want a sense of purpose that avoids despair, we need to dethrone all the idols that claim to calm the restless heart but which do not equal love. And if we aspire to true belonging, the only way to create it is love's exchange.

Augustine was right, of course.

One way of thinking about the essential brokenness of human nature from a Judeo-Christian perspective is that all of us are guilty of breaking the first of the Ten Commandments. All of us, at some level, worship gods we have created instead of the God who created us. In the modern age, those who say this tend to talk about wealth and power and status and pleasure as false gods (because there really aren't that many folks out there sacrificing to Ba'al these days).

The truth is, those who claim religious affiliation are just as prone to worshiping a version of the Biblical God that better soothes our consciences through selective editing. We all, for the most part, emphasize the aspects of God that align with what we already agree with, and minimize or forget the aspects of God that would make us change the way we live our lives.

The gods we prefer to worship, for the most part, seem better on the front end. Ultimately, they disappoint.

For most of my life, the god I worshiped was the one who said that there was a plan for me to fulfill some unique destiny. That I had one "life potential," and I just had to find out what it was and live into it.

A friend of mine asked me if I'd seen the show "The Big Door Prize" on Apple TV+. I'd seen the promos when it came out, but didn't pick it up until the friend mentioned it. But since I'm an amateur theologian who takes requests, and there are clearly some theological angles here, I jumped in.

The premise is that a mysterious machine shows up at a small-town five-and-dime that promises to reveal "your life potential" in exchange for two bucks (and your Social Security number and fingerprints, which sets off all my fraud-fighter alarm bells). People in the town grasp onto the little blue card that the MORPHO machine spits out for them with varying levels of intensity, but most of the show is about people making dramatic changes in their lives to drop what they've been doing — careers, marriages, you name it — and embrace what the machine says their true potential is.

I don't know, but this seems like a very American thing. Our culture leans into the myth of the "self-made" and lionizes the individual with a dream they pursue until the happy ending. It's enough to make you think that maybe we really do each have that one thing, that one true life potential, and our success and happiness in the world is just a reflection of how astutely we discerned what the thing was, and how persistent we were in pursuing it. If we aren't happy with our lives, maybe it's because we haven't found that true calling yet, or maybe it's because we gave up on our dream too soon.

What it took a lot of my life to figure out is, the god who orders life like that, the god who assigns one true life potential to each person and challenges us to play hide and seek to find it, that's just another false idol.

Augustine was right, way back in the fourth century. He opens his autobiographical *Confessions* by saying to God "You have made us for Yourself, O Lord, and our heart is restless until it rests in You."

God is not a MORPHO machine, nor does God hide our one true life potential for us to seek. It is we who hide, behind all the false gods, including the "true life potential" one.

But if God were to deliver us a blue envelope with a card inside that told us our one true life potential, they would all say the same thing:

LOVER/BELOVED

The rest — the vocations and passions and careers and hobbies — are for us to work out later. Not that God doesn't want to be part of that working out — I do believe there's a place for discerning whether a particular vocation is a better or worse way for you to practice the roles of lover and beloved. But those details are downstream from the one thing, the true life potential. Whether you live out your calling as a priest or a spouse, it's less about the specifics themselves than how they train you for letting your heart rest where it belongs.

S ometimes, idols hide, behind demons, inside wounds.

For most of my young adulthood — really, from when I was in college until I was almost 40 — if you had asked me what my "essential wound" was, as spirituality writers call it, I probably would have said that I was tormented by the idea that I was *supposed to have it all figured out, and I didn't.* (Even then, I would have recognized that this is the kind of "essential wound" that only a really privileged and lucky person could have.)

I'm not sure I even remember anymore how I got stuck on the idea that a person should know exactly what they were meant to do, from an early age, and then spend their lives striving after it. It probably stemmed from being a big sports fan, because almost every world-class athlete has a variation of this story: *At a very early age, I knew I wanted to be great at X, and I sacrificed everything else in my life to achieve it.* It's pretty rare that someone says, you know, I kind of messed around until I was about 20, and then all of a sudden I discovered that I was in the top 0.0001% of pitchers/shot-putters/breaststrokers. Generally, it takes an unhealthy, even idolatrous, commitment to a craft to be world-class, and *Sports Illustrated* only writes features about the world-class folks.

I guess to a degree, I was set up for this by my backstory. For as long as I can remember, I knew that I was adopted. The story I understood was that a couple, both college kids, got pregnant and knew they weren't ready for parenthood, so they put me up for adoption, to be taken in by a 40-something couple with four wonderful girls and a seat on the board of the local Children's Home, a wonderful family that decided they could handle one more.

When you mix this story with the reality that, had I been conceived five years later, legal abortion would likely have been a more attractive option for my would-be parents, it hardens into a rock-solid belief that I am here, when so many others are not, for a specific, heroic reason.

When your parents shower you with the mantra that you can be anything you want, and you marry that infinite range of possibility with the indistinct call to heroism, you get someone who spends a whole lot of time stressing about being off-course. Like, I'm supposed to be somewhere, I'm late, and I don't even have a clue where that somewhere is supposed to be. I really thought that this unguided call to heroism was the demon I had been assigned.

I was a lot of fun to hang out with, as you have no doubt discerned.

There are a couple of movies that come to mind here. I have watched *When Harry Met Sally* probably twenty times, and I never really identified with Harry Burns, but his quote about reading the last page of a book first because he wanted to know how it ends, in case he dies, was half-right for me. I wasn't focused on dying — few in their 20s and 30s are — but I wanted to know how it ended. And by "it," I meant "my life." It tormented me not to know.

But a less well-known movie I've also seen more than a dozen times is also on my mind. Late in *The Family Man*, protagonist Jack, played by Nicolas Cage says:

> *I feel like I'm living someone else's life. I remember I used to walk to work, and, uh, I had a warm bialy in my hand, and a hot cup of coffee from Dean & Deluca, the crisp feeling of The Wall Street Journal, the smell of leather from my briefcase. I used to be so sure about everything, confident. You know, I — I knew exactly who I was... and what I wanted.*

> *And then one morning, I woke up...and suddenly it was all different.*

> Kate (his wife, played by Tea Leoni) interjects: *Worse, do you mean?*

Jack: *No.*

Well, maybe a few things, but mostly just different. And it's okay.

But I never used to be like this, Kate. I was the guy who had it all figured out.

I had no doubts.

I had no regrets.

Kate: *And now?*

Jack: *Now I don't.*

I don't have it all figured out.

I obviously had never enjoyed the certainty of the first half of that monologue — I still don't know what a bialy is (a pastry, maybe?) — but that "lost-ness" that Jack has was definitely where I lived my young adulthood, and that certainty was where I was convinced I was supposed to be.

If single-mindedness is what breeds world champions and historical figures and saints, shouldn't it be appropriate that I was hungry for that? Where's the idol here?

Hiding.

An idol, at its essence, is something you put above God in the pecking order of your priorities, and having it all figured out was definitely more important to young-me than a relationship with God or almost anyone else. That shouldn't be a shocker — we cast heroes as solitary men on tops of mountains, not in the midst of relationship messiness.

Partly, my idol was an image of God who both had a master plan with all the details accounted for and who liked to play hide and seek with the people who lived out their lives in the unwitting fulfillment of that plan. Like watching rats in a maze, a distant God looked on with the certainty of where the paths lead, but without the compassion to clue in the rats. That God was either a scientist or a sadist, or both.

But the other part of this idol was about me, not God. I wanted to have it all figured out because only then, I would be able to be at peace. I didn't want to have to trust God, or anyone else. I was Missouri, a one-man "Show Me State." If you've seen the sign at the register "In God We Trust; All Others Pay Up Front," I didn't exempt God from that. I wanted to be able to trust in the plan that I figured out, or else nothing.

It's fitting that the two movie scenes that come to mind for me are both romantic comedies. Both show how life is centered not around accomplishments or even around storybook settings, but on the reality of mutual relationships. Slowly, and in fits and starts, I gave up on having it all figured out. But what finally wrested this idol from my hands was love.

That scene in The Family Man? Here's how it ends.

Kate asks: *What are you sure about?*

And Jack answers: *I'm sure that right now, there's nowhere else I'd rather be than here with you.*

Understanding The Assignment

"They understood the assignment."

That's been a popular phrase lately. I noticed it in social media posts about celebrities at the Met Gala who showed up in sufficiently avant-garde fashion choices, but I'm sure it long predates that (and will soon be passé). It calls to mind the kid who shows up to class having done the wrong homework, or the one who misreads the essay question on the exam. They *didn't* understand the assignment. These other folks did.

The academic element of this phrase is ironic, because when it comes to my mind, it's usually because someone thinks they can win the day by being the smartest person in the room, the kid with all the answers. A major part of our culture conflates academic success with success, period, and well, sometimes that's not the assignment. I remember being at a political debate once, when one candidate was clearly establishing himself as the "smart one." The other guy ceded that lane, instead positioning himself as the "normal one." And I knew, in that moment, that the "smart one" was going to lose, bad. He did, because he didn't understand the assignment. I've been a huge nerd for most of my life, and I remain an unabashed fan of learning. But more often than not, thinking you are the smart one in the room gets in the way of success rather than aiding it.

The ninth chapter of the Gospel of John tells that story. It's a healing story, well told, with interesting characters, and even some humor!

Fr. Raymond E. Brown's Anchor Bible Commentary on the Gospel of John is really helpful in highlighting the reversal of fates of the man born blind and the Pharisees. The Pharisees, confronted with this guy who was healed on the Sabbath (contrary to their rules), start with the certainty that they know what's what, and then they just dig deeper into their confidence that they have the right answer.

First, it's "This man (Jesus) is not from God because he does not keep the Sabbath," which gets some pushback.

Then, it's "We know that this man (Jesus) is a sinner."

Then, when the formerly blind guy argues with them, they turn on him: "You were born steeped in sin, and now you are lecturing us?"

By the end, Jesus is pointing out that while they claim they can see, they are really more blind than the other guy ever was. Because they started from a place of certainty, they lost the opportunity to learn.

What about the protagonist of the story? He starts from self-acknowledged ignorance and picks up momentum as he goes.

The first time he tells his friends what happens, all he knows about the guy who healed him is that he's "That man they call Jesus." When they ask where he is, he says, "I have no idea."

When he tells his story to the Pharisees and they ask who he thinks Jesus is, he takes a step forward. "He is a prophet."

And by the time he gets called back up to the stand, he's lecturing the experts. "We know that God pays no attention to sinners, but He does listen to someone who is devout and obeys His will. It is absolutely unheard of that anyone ever opened the eyes of a man born blind. If this man were not from God, he could have done nothing."

(And that's when he gets thrown out by the Pharisees.)

As I read the gospels, the recurring unpleasant realization I have is that I see myself (and the Church) a lot more in the Pharisees than I do in the people Jesus really connects with. When you're a Church Kid, you get rewarded for knowing the "right" answers about God, and it can seduce you into believing that that's what's really important. We in the West conflate faith with cognitive belief so much that you can be trapped into thinking that if you memorize all the rules and learn what's what, you'll pass a final quiz to get into heaven. The last judgment? St. Peter at the Pearly Gates? They're basically just oral exams.

But that isn't the assignment.

Unlike other healings, the man born blind doesn't ask Jesus to be healed. In fact, he doesn't speak at all until later. And when he does, he doesn't really know any of the answers that matter; he just knows he was healed. In fact, he says, "Whether he is a sinner, I do not know; one thing I do know: I was blind, and now I see." All the rest comes later.

That's the trick of it all. The good news is that there isn't really an assignment to understand at all. Accept good gifts we didn't even think to ask for. Be grateful and curious about the giver. Lean into all the things we don't know instead of leaning on what we think we do know. Remember that we're being invited to a family reunion, not a dissertation defense.

• • • •

Originally published November 2022

Hanna-Barbera Time

OK so let me tell you about Acts Chapter 19, because it has the only passage I ever preached on, which is also one of the cartooniest stories of the Bible. Over the almost 30 years (!) since I preached on it, I've come to realize a few things that put it in a different perspective. And none of this shows up in the lineup of readings that the Church uses at Mass, so you almost certainly have never noticed any of this. Pull up a chair, because this will take a minute.

When I was finding my way to seminary in 1991, my wife swears that I was still open to pastoral ministry, but even though her memory is much better than mine, I'm pretty sure I had discerned that being a preacher was not for me by the fall when I enrolled at Candler School of Theology in Atlanta. And here's why I know that:

As first-year divinity students, we had a small group class that went through supervised ministry together (which was as chaplains at a nursing home for the severely disabled, which is another story). As part of the initial ice-breaker/get-to-know-you exercises, we each had to preach a sermon to the class. I knew by that point that I wasn't going to be a preacher, and I never took a class on preaching, which may be why I never learned the recognizable cadence of the "UMC (United Methodist Church) pastor voice." But I still had to take my turn, so I preached on this story from Acts 19:11-20.

I reference Hanna-Barbera cartoons a lot when I talk about Acts, but this is specifically a Sylvester the Cat moment. Paul is continuing his "preach-til-you-get-beat-up" tour through the Mediterranean and has come to Ephesus (19:1-10). He is on a roll, at this point, so much so that "God did extraordinary miracles" through Paul, "so that handkerchiefs or aprons were carried away from his body to the sick, and the diseases left them and the evil spirits came out of them." (v. 11-12) It's almost like he was Elvis, or maybe Oprah.

There were working Jewish exorcists in town, seven brothers who traveled around throwing out demons, and they saw this hanky-healing as some next-level stuff. They figured, much like Mickey in The Sorcerer's Apprentice, "How hard can this be?" and they go to a guy with an evil spirit and say "I adjure you by the Jesus whom Paul preaches."

To which the evil spirit says, "Jesus I know, and Paul I know of. But you – who are you?" And the guy the spirit has inhabited rises up and beats the bejeezus out of all seven guys, who "fled out of that house naked and wounded." Whenever I read that, the image is always of Sylvester (or maybe Wile E. Coyote), bested by something he's clearly no match for, running to the hills with big patches of fur missing and Ace bandages wrapped around his bare-skinned wounds.

When I preached on that, it was with this message: you can fake a lot of stuff, but you can't fake God. Romantic that I was, I thought that if you were going to enter ordained ministry, it wasn't enough to have the skills for the job or the ambition to get ahead; ministry was something God had to actually *call* you to, or else you'd end up eventually like the sons of Sceva, butt-whipped, exposed, and running for the hills. And I was not *called* to ordained ministry. Amen. Next preacher.

I still believe that. I still believe that God calls people to ministry, and that there are a lot of folks who are tempted to try to fake it. I believe, even in the face of current evidence, that sooner or later, they're either going to come up against a God who doesn't recognize them or a demon who only defers to true holiness, and they're going to get their butt whipped. They will have deserved it.

Over the 30+ years since, though, I've realized some other stuff. 1) Whether we're called to official ministry or not, we can and must still take care of each other, which is what ministry is, really. 2) Whether we're called to official ministry or not, we should expect to feel like we aren't worthy, aren't ready, aren't up to the task, because we aren't. It's not Paul or his hankies that have the power; they're just hankies. It's the fact that God uses them (and him) that makes them something more. Same deal with us. 3) We might get thrashed like Sylvester because we are pretending to be something we aren't. But sometimes we get thrashed even when we're doing what we're supposed to be doing. Such is the nature of God's timeline versus ours, I guess. Many days, it looks to me like the arc of the moral universe doesn't bend at all. But in the long, long run, you can see where someone beaten on a bridge in Alabama or hung on a cross in Jerusalem can be a part of a redemptive story that just takes way too long to resolve for my impatient tastes.

Here's the other thing those three decades have taught me: the passage that is really important isn't the Sons of Sceva skit; it's the one after it. What sinks Paul in Ephesus is that he disrupts the economy and challenges the exceptionalism of Ephesus. You see, the Ephesians were known for being the home of the goddess Artemis. They had an economy built around making little Artemis statues for people to take home after they visited the Artemis shrine (for which they could book Fast Passes. Just kidding.) When Paul caught fire, he turned people against the idea that there was any god but God, and the local chamber of commerce realized that he was an existential threat. If people bought into this idea that God was the only god, they wouldn't come to Ephesus. They wouldn't buy the statues. If they were going to maintain Ephesian Exceptionalism, if they were going to Keep Ephesus Great, they needed to get rid of that Paul and his heresy.

The world we live in has its own versions of Artemis. Maybe they're political. Maybe they're economic. Maybe they're national, or racial. Maybe they deny that Paul's God is the real deal or maybe they just don't care. But they will kill to keep the illusion they worship safe.

Paul's world was so different from ours, but the dynamics are the same. Some people, like the Sons of Sceva, are going to try to co-opt the message of God so they can use that power for their own selfish ends. And some people, like the Ephesian silversmiths, are going to try to drive out any message of God that threatens to supplant the idols they make and sell. But in the end, you can't fake God. So keep ministering anyway, keep taking care of each other, whether you feel called or not.

. . . .

Originally published August 2020

Lord or Servant?

Here's something we have in common with 13th century Italy. Then as now, young men were steeped in a culture that glorified violence as the path to significance. If you wanted to be somebody as a guy back then, you wanted to be a knight, a warrior.

Giovanni Bernardone was no exception as a youth. To make something of himself, he took up arms and traveled to the next town to fight for his team. Off he went to war, battling the neighboring Perugians, which didn't go so well. He was captured, and spent a year in prison before his family paid his ransom, and it took a toll on him that left him in a funk of convalescence and doldrums for another year.

But back he went, because if you wanted to be a real man, you went out to fight. Pause and think about the stories in the last week, month, year, that center on young men primed for violence by the expectation that it was the noble thing to commit oneself to.

On his way back to battle, Giovanni had a dream, where he heard a question: "Would you rather serve the Lord or the servant?" And when he answered, "the Lord," he heard, "Then why are you trying to make the Lord into the servant?" And that's when he knew it was God, telling him that choosing to be a warrior was choosing something other than serving God.

And what about today? When you look at where people place their hearts, where we find meaning, we try to elevate a lot of things to the top spot that don't belong there. Pew says that Americans are far more likely than others to say that their spiritual life gives them meaning, but it's still about 15% of Americans who say that, and my guess is that for many of those 15%, their spiritual life revolves around a God that is enmeshed with their political party or race or country.

There is a lot to say about Giovanni, better known by his nickname Francesco, or Francis of Assisi, and peacemaking, but the first hurdle to face is this: what secondary goods, like country or politics, do we elevate above serving God and loving others?

This is another hard lesson from Francis. Look, my dad served in the armed forces twice, as a Marine pilot in World War II and as a Navy dentist during the Korean conflict. I have good friends who served our country in contemporary war zones, and friends with kids in the military today. I grew up playing Little League on a Navy base and watching *Red Dawn*. It is a challenge for me to say that military service is not a noble calling.

When Francis gave up his weapons, his primary impetus wasn't explicitly that God told him fighting was bad. But in some ways, what he heard was even more challenging, because the question he heard applies to all of us, regardless of whether or not we aspire to be warriors.

Every year, Catholics celebrate the Feast of Christ the King, and while that title is an old one, the feast wasn't instituted until 1925, by a pope who was concerned by the rise of secularism and nationalism in the world (and was maybe a little bitter that Italy had unified, shrinking Vatican power). It's still timely to ask ourselves, who are we serving with our lives? The master, or just a servant?

• • • •

Originally published November 2021

Pride

The Greatest That Ever Lived

All I want out of life is that, when I walk down the street, folks will say, "There goes the greatest hitter that ever lived." - Ted Williams, the greatest hitter that ever lived

How do you want to be known?

Achievement is a separate idol all its own. To be able to accomplish something significant is a cause that can supplant God as first in your heart, to be sure.

But celebrity is different. Celebrity isn't about what you do, it's about who you are. Or, rather who you are perceived to be.

Early in the Gospel of Mark, as Jesus is starting his ministry, there's a line that jumped out at me. After he amazes listeners with his teaching in the synagogue and evicts his first demon in Capernaum, Mark 1:28 says "And his fame went out quickly, throughout the entire region of Galilee."

If there's a part of you that goes "Ooh. I want that," you might want to hang around for this.

Fame, celebrity, is something that has sat on an altar for me, too. When I was a kid, I was a modestly competitive swimmer, and to this day, whenever the summer Olympics roll around, I find myself looking at the Olympic qualifying times and thinking, "Maybe I still have a shot." (SPOILER: I do not.)

Though I have returned to the pool as a 50-something, that Olympic lust isn't because I love swimming. Nor is it some great patriotism that makes me want to represent my country in competition. Nor is it the desire to be a part of something bigger than myself. It is nothing more than the desire, when I walk down the street, for folks to say "There goes an Olympic swimmer."

F. Scott Fitzgerald was known to have said that the rich are different than you and me, and I suspect he's right. But the *famous*, the ones people recognize when they walk down the street, are the ones that have gotten my envy over the years.

There is something captivating about the idea that people would know who you are and treat you like something special even if they'd never met you. I remember when I got married, the staff at the hotel where we spent the first night of our honeymoon answered the phone when my wife called down and referred to her as "Mrs. Johnson," which still makes her grin. Obviously, some of that is wedding giddiness, but it's also the magical feeling of being known by strangers for who you are. The thrill is (I suspect) not quite so great, but to this day, any customer service system that enables the first person answering the phone to call me by name without asking it impresses me. They know who I am.

While I was in seminary, I was an intern for the Atlanta Braves' chaplain. I remember the jitters I had when I worked with star players. My car once leaked on an All-Star. I had breakfast with the top relief pitcher in baseball once. I got marriage advice from a league MVP and a future Hall of Famer. When they walked down the street, or went for coffee, or just wanted to be left alone, people knew who they were.

But those players, and the gold medalists and movie stars and musicians and politicians I've met, all learned something very quickly after this phenomenon happened to them. Strangers knew who they were when they walked down the street. They might even know a lot about them. But those folks didn't really *know* them.

Many times in my life, I didn't so much switch gears as learn that what I thought I wanted wasn't really what I wanted at all. And that was the case with celebrity. Over time and exposure, I came to realize that people knowing who I was seemed like a validation that I was a really important person, that my life had worth, but it wasn't any more true than the idea that someone who knew what Ted Williams' batting average was actually knew Ted Williams.

Being truly known and loved is more meaningful and more powerful than any fame can deliver, it took me a while to figure out. The longer I live, the more I understand the value of a bunch of people knowing my name pales in comparison to the value of even one person knowing me personally. I'd rather walk down the street and have nobody notice me than have everyone know my name but nobody *know* who I really am.

At the pool where I swim, there are actually several legitimate Olympic swimmers, including a few gold medalists. One grew up swimming for the youth team based at the pool, and suddenly one day he went from being Bobby, one of the guys who used to swim here as a kid to Bobby Finke, American Record Holder and Olympic Gold Medalist. (To his great credit, he came back to the pool with his medals from Tokyo and Paris. He brought them to a kids' meet so they could see them and try them on themselves. I don't know him, but by all accounts of those who do, he has remarkably remained "Bobby from the pool" in his mind.)

It seems to me, like many of the other celebrities I have known, he must have figured out that it may sound great to be known, but it is far superior to be *known*.

My Misunderstanding

There's a funny misunderstanding in the life of St. Francis of Assisi that I got a new insight to during a recent retreat.

You might know Francis' story. He was praying in a little, rundown, abandoned church in the valley below Assisi, and the painting of Jesus on the crucifix spoke to him, by his account, saying "Francis, go rebuild my church, which as you can see is being destroyed." That crucifix is still around – it's in a chapel in the Basilica of Santa Chiara in Assisi, and you can pray in front of it, just like he did.

So Francis did what the man (well, the piece of centuries-old wood) said; he rebuilt the little, rundown, church, San Damiano. First he did it by stealing some of his dad's stuff, selling it, and giving the priest who ran the church the money. The priest, no fool, wouldn't take it. So Francis begged people for stones to use in rebuilding the church by hand, and he did it himself. He even got so carried away that he rebuilt two other little rundown churches in the area. You can go to San Damiano and sit in that same chapel, and you can go to one of the other little churches he rebuilt, called the Porziuncola, which sits inside the middle of a huge basilica, Santa Maria degli Angeli.

As cool as that is, Francis missed the point.

Over the course of Francis' life and mission, it became clear that the church that the crucifix told Francis to rebuild wasn't the decrepit little chapel, but the capital-C Church. He was called to something a lot bigger than he knew.

So, me? I apparently was called to something a lot smaller, I have learned.

I am always searching for how to prove myself, hunting for the specific way God is calling me to earn my existential keep. I have said this before, but I really think that being the result of an unwanted pregnancy, pre-Roe, has always left me aware of the many who have been similarly unwanted who have not had the gift of living. My whole life, I've been thinking that I must have made it to this point because God had some major thing for me to do. Maybe lead some people out of Egypt, or rebuild a capital-C Church. Something big enough to warrant being here.

In 2014, the first time my family and I really spent time in Assisi, I went to that crucifix and those little churches and I really wanted to hear what that something was. I mean, I was 45, and while I had kind of settled into a groove by that point, my head continued to be on a swivel, looking for whatever it was that God had put me here for.

The crucifix Jesus did not speak to me. Yeah, I was bummed, too.

I was talking with my spiritual director after I got back, and I told him about not getting any talking-crucifix messages, but that I kept feeling like there was something about being a peacemaker in all the time we spent there, and he said, well, maybe God is calling you to be a peacemaker.

That sounded pretty big, because, you know, look around. And I think when I got the inspiration to start a nonprofit I called Love Not Fear a couple years later, and when I really started digging into how to disrupt despair a few years after that, those were expressions of me trying to be a peacemaker, in the big sense.

I put the Love Not Fear organization to rest after a few years, because I just couldn't figure out how to make it into what it needed to be. And I never pulled together the big idea on disrupting despair. And, honestly, when we went back to Assisi for a more intense retreat, peacemaking had not been on my mind for a long time and was not part of the retreat plan at all.

Until it kept coming up. The first day we were there, being a peacemaker came back up in my prayer. The next day was a feast day, for Mary, Queen of Peace. The next day, the homilist at Sunday Mass preached on peace. The next day, U.S. Independence Day, the readings were all about peace, like, in an overabundant way. After which I noticed a prayer for peace from my favorite actual saint, Saint John

XXIII, in the prayer book. A couple days later, another reading I hadn't planned was on peacemaking. That kind of thing makes you laugh after a while, and I laughed a lot.

But along with that came a message that was the opposite of what Francis dealt with in the whole church-rebuilding misunderstanding:

Think small.

A couple of the other main messages I got in that retreat?

- To make peace, be at peace.
- To be at peace, consider yourself nothing.
- To consider yourself nothing, be in love with the Ultimate Something.

Not "write a book." Not "resuscitate the 501c3." Not "launch a social movement."

Be at peace. Go deeper with God. Invest deeply in your relationships. The nonscalable stuff.

My misunderstanding.

• • • •

Originally published July 2022

I Feel Bad for Michael Jordan

I feel bad for Michael Jordan.

Jordan, of course, is one of the greatest basketball players in the history of the sport and one of the clutch performers of all time in any sport. You probably have heard the story that he did not make the varsity team during his sophomore year of high school; his coach picked Jordan's friend, Leroy Smith, instead. (Smith was 6-foot-7 to Jordan's then-5-10.) That snub drove Jordan's pursuit of excellence throughout his career, so much so that when Jordan was inducted into the Basketball Hall of Fame, he invited Smith to attend the ceremony, told the story, and pointed out that, while Smith's stopped growing and didn't get any better as a player, Jordan became, well, Jordan.

I know people – a lot of people, actually – who similarly use a past failure, snub or trauma to motivate them. The same way that Jordan worked so hard to master his craft, just so he could say to the high school coach, "You made a mistake, dude," these people work so that they can go back to whoever slighted them and rub it in their face. They're just not as famous or successful as MJ.

I was talking with a close friend the other day who knew this story and has said that they hope to be able to do something similar (on a smaller scale) – to be able to achieve something that enables them to show their doubters how wrong they were. And because they are a close friend, I was able to tell them something that they didn't want to hear, something I don't think Michael Jordan has admitted but I suspect learned the day after his Hall of Fame induction.

Revenge won't make you whole. Proving the haters wrong won't bring you peace.

I appreciate that on the surface it seems pretty silly to feel bad for Michael Jordan, since by every earthly measure he's a remarkably successful human being. But to devote your whole life to a cause, achieve it, and then recognize that it was a cause that wasn't worth the work is a tragedy.

I told my friend something that I expected they would not be able to really accept for a long time, but hoped they would remember: that the path to wholeness and peace isn't revenge, but forgiveness, whether it's merited or not.

I told them that this is one of those things that sets apart true Christianity. There are other religions that will counsel you to let go of those slights and snubs and release that negative energy, but actually forgiving someone who does you wrong, whether or not they are repentant, seems like something you would only think to do if you have a constant reminder of Jesus forgiving the people who crucified him.

The reality is, I doubt Michael Jordan's high school coach thought much of his roster decision at the time, and in my friend's case, I am pretty sure that the people who slighted them have no memory of doing so. Whether my friend forgives them or not is entirely irrelevant to them, because they aren't a part of my friend's life.

But it will matter to my friend. Revenge is a form of hatred turned into action, and that action drives choices that over time, will make you a harder, pettier, less kind version of who you can be. If you let it become your focus, it can drive you to excellence and achievement. But only by ensuring that you never, ever, feel whole and never, ever, experience peace.

I hope my friend learns that message earlier rather than later; hopefully it won't wait until they are on an awards show stage to sink in. As much as we need excellence, there are other paths to get there. And what the world seems to have a greater shortage of than champions like Jordan is people who are whole, healed, and at peace. Those are the folks who can really transform the world.

"You're off the list!"

When I worked with the Tampa Bay Rays, there was a guy in our sales group who, whenever he was upset with someone for some small grievance, would bellow "You're off the list," and summarily cross them off of his interoffice phone list. This happened a lot, almost always for pretty inconsequential stuff, and was mostly a joke to him and to everyone else. He never really reinstated people formally to "the list," but I think he reprinted his phone list from time to time. (Also, we were all in the same room, so it's not like we really needed phones to talk to each other.)

There has probably always been an element within Christianity that has sought to restrict who's "on the list" as a believer; in Acts, you see the early Church going rounds about whether non-Jewish believers can join the group without first converting to Judaism. It's ebbed and flowed since then, I suspect, and I'm sure that there are scholars who can identify what elements in a given time and place breed a stronger instinct to shorten the list.

History tells us that right now is probably not the worst it's ever been on this front, but it's a little disquieting to realize that the phrase "more Catholic than the pope," once a hyperbolic joke, lacks its former punch, as you see stories about American Catholic seminaries full of students who disavow the current pope to such a degree that there are declared "Francis-free" zones. (I don't know if this kind of "who counts" list-keeping is as much a thing in Protestant and evangelical circles.)

In his letter, James defines "religion that is pure and undefiled before God, the Father, is this: to care for orphans and widows in their distress, and to keep oneself unstained by the world." (1:27) That first part, most people can wrap their heads around and get onboard with, but the second part can be read a lot of different ways. The writers of the New Testament and generations of interpreters have layered a lot onto what in "the world" we need to keep free from, and I have my own biases on that front just like everyone else. But a couple points from James' letter might be helpful.

James's framing of the law hinges on love of neighbor (2:8). Earlier, he uses some uncharacteristically frilly language to talk about what it means to act from a place on "God's list": "Every generous act of giving, with every perfect gift, is from above, coming down from the Father of lights, with whom there is no variation or shadow due to change. In fulfillment of his own purpose he gave us birth by the word of truth, so that we would become a kind of first fruits of his creatures. You must understand this, my beloved: let everyone be quick to listen, slow to speak, slow to anger, for your anger does not produce God's righteousness. Therefore rid yourselves of all sordidness and rank growth of wickedness, and welcome with meekness the implanted word that has the power to save your souls." (1:17-21).

Quick to listen, slow to speak. Slow to anger, meek.

A couple chapters later, after talking about how perilous the tongue can be (and how dangerous teaching can be), he comes back to what it looks like to be unstained by the world. "Show by your good life that your works are done with gentleness and born of wisdom. But if you have bitter envy and selfish ambition in your hearts, do not be boastful and false to the truth...the wisdom from above is first pure, then peaceable, gentle, willing to yield, full of mercy and good fruits, without a trace of partiality and hypocrisy. And a harvest of righteousness is sown in peace for those who make peace." (3:13-18)

Gentleness and peace. Full of mercy and good fruits (which aren't enumerated here. Paul has my favorite list in Galatians 5:22-23).

The New Testament doesn't really have a clear manual for what a church is supposed to do or what it's for, but at the end of some letters, you get a flurry of things that, taken together, look kinda sorta like an outline of what church looks like. Paul does it in I Thessalonians 5, for instance, and so James does here:

"Are any of you suffering? They should pray. Are any cheerful? They should sing songs of praise. Are any among you sick? They should call for the elders of the church and have them pray over them, anointing them with oil in the name of the Lord. The prayer of faith will save the sick, and the Lord will raise them up; and anyone who has committed sins will be forgiven. Therefore confess your sins to one another, and pray for one another, so that you may be healed." (5:13-16) Then after a quick example of the power of prayer, he closes the letter abruptly with "My brothers and sisters, if anyone among you wanders from the truth and is brought back by another, you should know that whoever brings back a sinner from wandering will save the sinner's soul from death and will cover a multitude of sins." (5:19-20) Not even a "the end" after that.

So James outlines a community that prays, praises, comforts and heals the sick, confesses and forgives sins, and especially reels back in those who wander away. That's the charge of the church, within an ethic of gentleness, peace, listening, humility.

The world, and even the Church, may be saying that we should be focused on crossing people off the list. But James seems to say here that God's not the one pushing us to take people off the list. He's asking us to help get people back on it.

· · · ·

Originally published August 2020

Andrew

He might be a dark horse candidate, but if I could pick one apostle to meet and talk with, it might be Andrew. And I'd ask him about the journey he must have gone through of burying his ego.

In the synoptic Gospels (Matthew, Mark and Luke), Andrew and (Simon) Peter get chosen together, brothers summoned from their job fishing for their father into discipleship. The Gospel of John ups the ante a little; Andrew is a follower of John the Baptist who goes (with a partner) to find out why John was so high on Jesus. He switches rabbis and brings his brother along. In the Orthodox tradition, Andrew is known as the first disciple for this.

But by the Gospel of Mark's ninth chapter, Jesus picks three of his twelve to go up the mountain alone with him (to witness the transfiguration, as it turns out). And (spoiler alert) he picks the same three to pray with him in the Garden of Gethsemane after the Last Supper. Peter...and the other pair of brothers, James and John.

How does that conversation go? How do you go from first disciple to the guy whose brother gets picked for all-stars while you stay on the bench? What must that have felt like?

Tradition has it that Andrew got over it, if it ever bothered him in the first place. He preached the Gospel around the Black Sea and other places. He is the patron saint of Romania, Ukraine and Russia, and was crucified (allegedly on an x-shaped cross) for believing in Jesus.

But what was that process of letting go of ego like? What was it like to be one of the "other 9," even though you were first to the party and brought along a brother who became the right-hand man?

That would be an interesting story to hear.

• • • •

Originally published August 2020

Control

Calendar Man

It started with a picture on a calendar.

One of the things that the advent of digital photography has brought is the ability for normal people to put together their own calendars. While it used to be that mall kiosks would spring up each November with rows and rows of calendars — of dog breeds or cars or football teams or country fields — which we would peruse to find the wall calendar that would accompany us through the next year, now, those of us who still use paper calendars can design our own, with photos from our own lives.

Both sides of our family have people who produce beautiful, family-focused calendars most years, and the companies that produce them offer templates that allow designers to put pictures, not only above the calendar, but on particular days. So, on your birthday, you are likely to have a picture of yourself, if your family member is savvy enough to navigate that.

My birthday is in January, so I see this right away. One year, probably around 2006 or 2007, we put up the calendar, and something about the picture in the square of my birthday unsettled me. Specifically, the number of chins I had. (It wasn't a particularly unflattering picture, mind you. None of this is the calendar-maker's fault.) And as I looked at that photo at the beginning of the new year, I resolved to do something about it.

At the time, I think I weighed just shy of 200 pounds. So I started exercising — first some stretching, then some walking, then swimming, the sport I had done in high school some 20 years earlier. Along with exercise, I identified a list of healthy foods and started shaping my diet toward them. And together, it turns out diet and exercise will affect your weight.

Since some of you may be interested in this kind of thing, what I actually did was build a list of healthy foods — fruits, vegetables, proteins, whole grains, etc. — and tracked each day how many different healthy foods I would eat. (I found that some of the juice smoothies they sell at the grocery store can have 7-8 different healthy foods in them, so that became my default lunch.) I also tracked whether I drank 64 ounces of water every day. I tracked how many times I swam (for at least 45 minutes) each week, with a goal of 150 workouts a year (which is three times a week). Eventually, I started waking up at 4:30 a.m. to swim before work, which meant I started going to bed around 9 p.m., even though I have never been a morning person and it meant going to bed before my wife did. And I weighed myself every day, tracking each day whether I was up or down over the previous day, over the previous week, over the previous month.

By taking control of all those variables, I was able to get measurable results, and I found that very, very attractive. After I dropped 40 pounds, getting down to about 157, my doctor told me to cut it out. She thought I needed to carry a little more weight on me to be healthy. But losing all that excess weight while developing a "swimmer's build" of broader shoulders tapering to a thinner midsection made me feel good about myself.

The thing is, even when I had dropped below the weight that my doctor considered healthy, I still saw opportunities to lose more. What started out as vanity — ensuring that next year's birthday picture would have only one chin — opened me up to a more pervasive idol, control. Even though I wasn't fully satisfied with how I looked, I was very satisfied with the power of being able to control those variables and shape myself, literally.

It didn't last. My job required more travel and more social engagements that made it harder to maintain the pace of exercise and diet. And that turned out to be a blessing.

Control turned into an idol for me. The warning signs that I missed were when I put my regimen above time with family and friends. The results of self-control can be rewarding, but the process is isolating in ways that are no good for anyone.

I got my extra chin back eventually. I've been up and down the scale a few times over the years, and I still track my exercise and weight while trying to eat well. But I've traded in the idol of control in order to balance those healthy behaviors with others, like prayer time, socializing, enjoying a good meal, spending time with my wife and daughter. Sometimes, I'm conscious of the tradeoffs I'm making in the moment, and sometimes I only realize later that staying up late for an important conversation means scrapping my morning swim. I don't beat myself up over that when it happens.

I've never really thought I was approaching full OCD; I know people who have struggles with that, and I wouldn't insult them by comparing my dalliance with control and their daily demon. But my experience opened my eyes to the fact that control is an idol, and I am happy to be rid of it, even if it means an extra chin.

I put myself in timeout yesterday afternoon. The dog made me do it.

We have a very old, almost completely blind and deaf Shih Tzu named Emmie. She sleeps even more than the usual dog, and between her age and her infirmities, she doesn't move very much. When she does move, it is at a very slow, tentative pace, to avoid smacking into a wall. Despite all that, she has a very sweet temperament; we have to administer all sorts of medication and treatments, including eye ointments and ear medicine, and she has never growled, snarled, or otherwise shown anger. And with one exception, when she wandered to a part of the house that was off-limits and got lost, she only barks in her sleep.

How, you may wonder, can I blame such an inoffensive animal for making me put myself in timeout?

As sweet as she is, Emmie does not handle stress well. While it's true that she neither barks nor bites nor runs in circles, stress will cause her to lose control of her bodily functions. Let me be more specific: she will poop on the floor when she's upset.

When the house needs a good cleaning, my job is to take Emmie into my study and keep her there until the cleaning is over. Since my goal is to make the study a poop-free zone, this means keeping her occupied and stress-free or, alternatively, holding on to her so she doesn't release her stress and other things. Hopefully.

How does one entertain a mostly immobile and sensory-limited, non-food-motivated dog whose only hobby is sleeping? Good question! In recent weeks, the strategy has been to create an "inactivity gym" — basically a collection of beds, blankets, sheets and towels that offer different surfaces on which to sleep. This has worked — there have been days where she finds a new thing on which to sleep and promptly starts snoring — but it isn't foolproof. If she is aware enough that her life has been disrupted, she will wander all over the room, seemingly purposefully avoiding the surfaces intended to give her comfort (which are also the surfaces that are easiest to clean). At which point I have to resort to "forced cuddling," which is not as much fun for either of us as it might sound. She does not bark or growl, but she does squirm and grumble.

Yesterday afternoon, this was the path Emmie chose, and for roughly 45 minutes, I found myself restraining a dog in my lap who very much did not want to be there. And it frazzled me so much that after everything had settled down, I had to go lie down in a dark room for an hour or so to recover from the stress.

Charitably, I could say that my frazzling came from empathy. It could be that the stress of not being able to provide comfort to another creature in distress just exhausted me. That could offer a great bridge to reflect on how we are all like Emmie sometimes, freaking out and losing our literal stuff over things that in the light of perspective don't warrant that response, rejecting options that would allow us more constructive ways to weather the storms of disruption, refusing to be comforted. I could even point to divine compassion, and how God became one of us in order to show us a better way to navigate life, only to be rejected by our unwillingness to let go of our stress and trust in God's providence.

But that wasn't really what this was about.

The truth is, I had plans for that hour that were based on Emmie being OK in the inactivity gym. My meltdown wasn't about compassion for Emmie; it was about my battle to stay in charge of my life. I spent that time holding the dog in one hand and trying to do a few more work tasks on the computer, which is what I had budgeted that time for. Doing both things poorly, which, let's face it, is the definition of multitasking, just wore me out. If I had been willing to surrender control over my life, and my to-do list, for just 45 minutes, I would probably have been in a better place.

And that, my friends, is a metaphor I can apply to most of my life. I have plans. I have stuff to do. I have an agenda. And when life disrupts those plans, I try to push through anyway.

We are wired to be in control of our lives. At least I am. Whenever we're confronted with a reality that asks us to recognize that that control is an illusion, it's stressful. Even when that reality is packaged as a Shih Tzu. Perhaps a part of the process of spiritual maturity is the intentional surrender of control. (Unfortunately, spiritual maturity isn't a reasonable expectation for dogs.) I'm going to have to learn, one of these days, to say "Take, Lord, and receive all my liberty…"

And next time, I'm just going to take Emmie outside and let her do whatever she wants.

What If He Thinks We Mean It?

I just finished Fr. Mark Thibodeaux's excellent *Ascending with Ignatius: A 30-Day At-Home Retreat*, which I recommend highly. He ends the last day with a prayer that St. Ignatius of Loyola, founder of the Jesuits, is known for:

Take, Lord, and receive all my liberty, my memory, and my understanding, and my entire will,

All that I have and call my own.

You have given all to me. To you, Lord, I return it.

Everything is yours; do with it what you will.

Give me only your love and your grace, that is enough for me.

I can pray that, so long as I'm reasonably sure that God's not going to take me up on the offer. But what if He thinks we mean it?

All the stuff we claim as ours, all the things we say we've done, they're really all given to us. And our calling is to offer them back to God, and mean it. This is the essence of what Jesuits call detachment, which is an attitude not of not caring, but of not being so attached to anything, even if you care about it, that that thing will keep you from following Jesus.

Hurricane Ian went through Florida recently, and while we don't live in an evacuation zone, big hurricanes like this still make you stare down the possibility that you might have to walk away from all you have called your own. Whether you're driving to higher ground or putting the tools away after affixing the last sheet of plywood, there is a point at which you look back at the house and everything inside it and realize that it might be taken by wind or water, and you realize that you are not so perfectly detached. You might really lose all this stuff that you said wasn't really yours anyway. And you really didn't mean it.

Hurricanes make that a reality for a lot of people all at once. So many people here in Florida have lost their homes. But it happens to other people every day in quieter ways. Dementia takes people's memories and understanding. Illness and addiction take people's life and liberty. War and famine make people walk away from their homes, just like hurricanes do.

The prayer ends positively: Give me only your love and grace, that is enough for me. And this is the opportunity in tragedy for those of us who dodged this particular bullet: to realize that the "love and grace" part is our job. Since we all belong to each other, we owe it to each other to provide the love and grace people need when they've lost all the other stuff.

Whether it's a storm or a war or a disease or a crime that makes them give up what they thought was theirs, it's our job, this time, to fill those gaps with love and grace. Whether they are in a hurricane shelter or a refugee camp or a memory care center or a prison, our job is to give them love and grace until they believe that that's enough. Just as we will rely on the same from others next time, when it's us.

· · · ·

Originally published October 2022

Make a Mess

Make a mess, but then also help to tidy it up. A mess which gives us a free heart, a mess which gives us solidarity, a mess which gives us hope. - Pope Francis, speaking to young people in Paraguay, 2015

In sports, you usually don't win if you're playing not to lose.

In life, you usually don't learn, or create, or connect if you're petrified of making a mistake.

In our moral life, you usually don't love if you're obsessively focused on not sinning.

I listen to podcasts a lot when I drive, and lately most of them have either been in Italian or are about learning Italian or both. This week as I was driving, one of the podcasters was saying (in English) that in order to really learn Italian, you have to speak it. What keeps Italian students from getting better is the fear that they will say the wrong thing.

"Like speaking Italian, you can't learn the guitar by reading books about music theory and practicing chords once a week. You have to play the guitar," she said. "You can't wait until you have everything perfect before you start, because you never will. You have to be willing to make mistakes or you'll never start. You learn more from your mistakes than from anything you study anyway."

And I thought, "This is not just about Italian and guitar, is it?"

When I am too tired for podcasts, I like listening to Scott Bradlee's music. Bradlee is the founder of Postmodern Jukebox, which takes pop songs and recasts them into different genres in ways that, virtually every time, improve on the original. Bradlee is a ragtime jazz pianist, and the constantly changing collection of musicians around him are all remarkable, but every once in a while, Bradlee gets to show what he can do on the piano, and if you can listen past the vocals to hear it, it is magical.

I can't believe there is sheet music for what he does. Bradlee doesn't play the "right notes." His playing is all over the map and literally all over the keyboard. But it fits the song perfectly and takes it to another level. Listen to his cover of "Call Me Maybe." Or "Stacy's Mom." (I know.) Or listen to the piano on Jason Robert Brown's "King of the World" from his Broadway show "Songs for a New World." The ability to play all around the "right notes" in a way that is both utterly chaotic and yet still spot-on just astounds me.

In order to be that creative, a musician has to have been okay making a lot of mistakes along the way. They have to have been willing to sound really foolish while they figured out what worked and what very much did not.

I think this is what Pope Francis was getting at when he told a group of young people to go "make a mess," early in his pontificate. (Which is a radical thing for a pope to say.)

I am struck by the way that Christians have taken a message proclaimed as Good News because of its offer of divine forgiveness and grace, looked past Jesus' clear moral direction to love whole-heartedly, everybody, always (to borrow from Bob Goff), and instead build a morality around the imperative for individuals to avoid sin. Sin is bad, yes. We should avoid it, yes. But if we focus all our energies on avoiding sin, we can handicap our ability to love.

Let me try another analogy. I have tried to lose weight over the years (some days I try harder than others). When I have been successful, it is not because I focused on what *not* to eat. The only diet that has ever worked for me is one that focuses on what healthy foods *to* eat, which has the effect of leaving less room and interest for the other, less healthy stuff.

You can make a moral system the same way. You can focus on finding new and powerful ways to live love – of God and neighbor –

until you find you have less time and inclination to focus on yourself (and self-absorption is where sin tends to come from anyway). But we, who were commanded to love, focus on building a system of not messing up instead.

It's funny that this was on my mind during a week when the Scripture readings for Sunday mass set up for a lot of "Stand up against sin" sermons. Ezekiel (33:7-9) has God telling Ezekiel that if he gets the message that God is going to smite someone, but he doesn't pass that message along, God will hold Ezekiel as accountable as the smited. Matthew (18:15-20) has Jesus telling his followers how to discipline members of the group who sin against each other. Even the response from Psalm 95 is "Harden not your heart," presumably if you get confronted by Ezekiel or fellow church members for doing something wrong.

But the theme of the psalm really isn't about scowling at sin. It's about joy, which doesn't stem from a scowl. And then Paul, in Romans 13:8-10, underscores the point:

Brothers and sisters: Owe nothing to anyone, except to love one another; for the one who loves another has filled the law.

I am not one of those progressives who doesn't believe sin is real. I know my own brokenness well enough to see it reflected around me. We are not OK. But there are a couple of reasons I think centering a morality on stamping out sin is the wrong way to pursue holiness.

First, it puts the light of the Good News under a basket. If the message we're supposed to spread is one of God's grace, we can't use all of our breath to tell people how to make themselves less awful. If we do, we end up misleading people into thinking Christianity is defined by a moral legalism that sounds a lot more like what Jesus yelled at the Pharisees for teaching than it does His own message.

Second, it's not successful, at least not as a centerpiece for sanctification. Have I changed some of the ways I live because I've tried to sin less? I have, at least to a degree, but only as a downstream effect of being touched by Love and wanting to reciprocate. If reducing sin was my main strategy, I would never find my way to Love; I'd just keep playing ethical whack-a-mole. The best way to avoid hell is to focus on pursuing heaven.

Third, to the extent anyone is paying attention to the message, it actually exacerbates what is emerging as the biggest challenge of the next generation: paralysis by fear. Look at the data around youth and young adults today, and the sins our parents harangued us to avoid – sex and drinking and even dancing are in decline (Loved *Footloose* as a teen, not gonna lie).

Yet isolation, loneliness, self-harm and suicide are on the rise among those same generations. At least some researchers point to the smartphone and social media as the culprits here, because they have created a fear of being ridiculed or even "canceled" that is so strong that many young people shrink from the world around them.

This is a secularized, high-tech version of centering morality on fear of sin over pursuit of love. The sins that get you ridiculed (awkwardness) or canceled (speaking your mind) might be different, but the focus on avoiding the bad is the same. Moreover, this secularized version lacks any assurance of grace, forgiveness or redemption. A sin-centered Christian morality feeds into the same ethos that creates the despair from which today's youth need saving.

None of the kids who are afraid of being imperfect are going to play piano like Scott Bradlee. They will never take the chance it requires to start speaking Italian poorly. Nor will they love like the saints. Even if Gen X kids like me grew up making messes and needed some reining in, the world has changed. Pope Francis was right, and radical. We need to encourage young people to make a mess (and then tidy it up).

If Love is anything, it is messy.

Not What I Ordered

What does it mean to be grateful for a gift that wasn't what you asked for?

In my defense, I have been on both sides of the story I'm about to tell.

My beloved, in an act of angelic generosity, went to get me coffee recently. But it wasn't made the way I would have ordered it.

Now, a decent person would have been so grateful for the gift of coffee that they would have wisely not said anything about it not being what they would have ordered. However, some of us, those without a filter, may have blurted out "That's not the way I like it," before almost-but-not-quite-instantaneously recognizing the words that leapt from their undercaffeinated mouth and trying desperately to reel them in, perhaps even physically pawing at the air to try to catch them before reaching the ears of their beloved gift-bearer.

Anyone who has had a young child in their life knows what it is to get a gift they didn't really want or need. Such is the nature of virtually every elementary school art project. We know, in that context, that it is the intent that counts, and the fact that it comes from this little person we love transcends any objective measure of beauty, craftsmanship or utility. What a gorgeous paperweight, honey, we say, and at some level we sort of mean it.

Yet there are things that matter to us deeply, like coffee, things we want to be *just the way we like it*, and when we get those things as gifts, we do the evaluation immediately of whether or not this gift is what we ordered. To our detriment, peril and shame, sometimes.

So, let's be real. Most of our lives are filled up with gifts that aren't what we ordered. How we respond – gratitude or "Excuse, me, miss?" – comes to define our character. We are all only truly humble to the degree that we are appropriately grateful. To parents that may not have done everything perfectly, but who did the best they could. To bodies that may not be Adonic, but are at least mostly healthy. To circumstances that didn't break exactly in our favor, but got us to an okay place. To a God who isn't a wish-fulfilling genie but gives us what we need, even if we aren't always so sure.

Whenever I would go to a movie with my parents, and later with my friends, one of the first questions afterward was always "What would you have done differently?" which helped form my critical mind. I can always tell you what I would have *rather* had. I would have chosen a God who didn't get crucified. I would have chosen a Gospel that wasn't so insistent on taking care of the outcast... except when I'm the outcast. I would have chosen Aladdin's genie.

And when I order healing, I am pretty specific. When I order peace, I have a particular arrangement in mind. When I order happiness, I want it to look just so.

The stuff I get from life? From God? A lot of the time, maybe most of the time, it's not really what I ordered. And yet it is still a gift to be grateful for.

When St. Francis of Assisi was drawing up his Rule of Life for his followers, one of the things he insisted on was "I beg the sick brother to thank God for everything and to desire to be whatever the Lord wills, whether sick or well." (Rule of 1221)

Everything. Sick or well, whichever.

It's worth pointing out that when he wrote the "Canticle of the Creatures," the beautiful prayer of gratitude to God for creation, he was sick unto death and absolutely miserable. He walked the talk on that one.

Me, I still have room to grow. I'm super grateful when my coffee order is right, and I'm working on the rest.

· · · ·

Originally published September 2022

Hey, let me tell you what I learned from my time playing a "pool boy."

I first really learned about intention by taking an acting class.

Don't get me wrong; by the time I got to college, I had heard many pep talks about going "all in." In sports, at church, at school, commitment is a common theme.

I am generally more of a "some in" kind of guy. I work or play hard, but I don't live and die on the outcomes. That's more true as I age, but even as a kid, I remember getting odd looks because, even though I played hard to win, I would also compliment an opponent who made a great shot or had an impressive swim. I had teammates who would go home crying after a loss; I can remember the times I was despondent after a defeat, but they weren't that often, and they taught me that being all-in can make you unbearable.

In this acting class, we focused a lot on intention. A lot of people make fun of actors who take themselves too seriously asking what their motivation is in a scene, and deservedly so, because actors can take themselves way too seriously. Until you try acting a scene with real intention.

For example, there was a scene where I played a pool boy. (It's OK. You can laugh.) You learn the lines, you learn the blocking, it's fine. Then the director guides you to identify the character's intention in the scene, and this character's intention was clearly to kiss the girl. And as I acted out that same scene that my partner and I had rehearsed into the ground, it played very differently. All of a sudden, what had been a kind of silly little skit had power. That was when I realized that living with intention had real power.

That was decades ago, and I still go back to that experience of acting a scene with intention and apply it to my life. When I do any sort of exercise, I mostly go through the motions or let my mind wander or focus on counting reps, but then once in a while I have the clarity to really do the thing with intention, whether it's swimming or push-ups or whatever, and I lock in my focus on making the most out of that lap or rep, and it makes a huge difference. Mostly it makes my muscles hurt or lungs ache in ways that they don't normally.

I see this in my spiritual life, too. I go through the motions on a whole bunch of the stuff Christians are supposed to do. I can read a Bible passage, put the book down, and have no recollection of a single word I just read. I can sit down to pray for someone or about something, and within seconds, I am on to something else. I can go to Mass, participate by saying all the things, doing all the actions, listening to the homily, and walk out with no real memory of anything happening. It's like magic.

But I also have times where I approach prayer, study, worship, or action with real intention, and I hold that focus without wavering, and I am deeply moved by the experience. I've decided that intention is the real difference maker in our lives, and if I had the presence to live each moment with a fidelity of intention, my life would be radically better.

Unless the intention is too small and becomes an idol.

I wrote earlier about my idol of vanity, and how it was really about control. Maybe at its heart, the idol was the commitment to a too-small intention. That's not one I have shaken.

I write this shortly after the new year, and I am one who doesn't make resolutions, but definitely takes time at the turn of the year to reflect and set new goals for the coming year. This year, I set a fitness goal, and I set a goal of becoming more fluent in Italian, so I can more fully engage when we travel there. These are two goals I have set with intention, and I know I will achieve them, God willing.

But I also know that God cares a lot less about my physical shape or my Italian fluency than He does my relationship with Him and with those He gives me to love. And I know that, while I would rather spend time loving God, my wife, my daughter and my friends, setting an intention on a measurable goal, like fluency or fitness, with concrete actions I can take to achieve it, creates the idol. If I am not very careful, I will ditch time with God and family to knock out some more Italian lessons. When a friend needs to connect over lunch, I will focus more on whether the menu has healthy options than on the needs of my friend. That is how intention works. Saying "yes" to your intention is saying "no" to a bunch of others.

So I can idolize my own ego by refusing to commit myself to something that might let me down, or I can idolize a small intention by committing what God and others deserve.

Whether you're playing a pool boy or living life, apparently, you need to figure out that some things are worth going all-in for, then make sure you go all-in for the right ones.

Relationship

A parable about a peasant runs along these lines:

There once lived a peasant in Crete who deeply loved his life. He enjoyed tilling the soil, feeling the warm sun on his naked back as he worked the fields, and feeling the soil under his feet. He loved the planting, the harvesting, and the very smell of nature. He loved his wife and his family and his friends, and he enjoyed being with them, eating together, drinking wine, talking, and making love. And especially he loved Crete, his beautiful island! The earth, the sky, the sea —-they were his! This was his home.

One day he sensed death approaching. What he feared was not what lay beyond, for he knew God's goodness and had lived a good life. No, he feared leaving Crete, his wife, his children, his friends, his home, and his land. And so, as he prepared to die, he grasped in his right hand a few grains of soil from his beloved Crete and told his loved ones to bury him with it.

He died, awoke, and found himself at heaven's gate, the soil still in his hands and heaven's gate firmly barred against him. Eventually Saint Peter emerged through the gates and spoke to him: "You've lived a good life, and we've a place for you inside, but you cannot enter unless you drop that handful of soil. You cannot enter as you are now!"

Reluctant to drop the soil, the man protested, "Why? Why must I let go of this soil? Indeed, I cannot! Whatever is inside those gates, I have no knowledge of. But this soil, I know. It's my life, my work, my wife and children, it's what I know and love, it's Crete! Why should I let it go for something I know nothing about?"

Peter answered, "When you get to heaven you will know why. It's too difficult to explain. I am asking you to trust, trust that God can give you something better than a few grains of soil."

But the man refused. In the end, silent and seemingly defeated, Peter left him, closing the large gates behind. Several minutes later the gates opened a second time and this time, a young child emerged. She did not try to coax the man into letting go of the soil in his hand. She simply took his hand and, as she did, it opened and the soil of Crete spilled to the ground. She then led him through the gates.

A shock awaited him as he entered heaven. There, before him, lay all of Crete!

- Our one great act of fidelity, Ronald Rolheiser 110-111

The best things are the most powerful idols.

When I was a younger, more immature young groom, marriage provided a different sort of idol. I hadn't had a lot of meaningful long-term romantic relationships before I met my wife, so when we were dating, and even in the early years of our marriage, I had to put to rest a series of common idols.

One was liberty. Every "yes" is a "no"; that is, any whole-hearted and intentional yes to something or someone means closing off other options. If I have a dollar, and I spend it here, I can't spend it again anywhere else. If I have an hour, and I spend it with you, I've closed off the ability to spend it elsewhere.

At points in our dating life, I wrestled with that. Probably because I hadn't had a lot of other girlfriends, I went through times of wondering whether my now-wife was "the right one," if there might be other, better options out there. In our culture, which has such a consumerist ideal of "shopping around for the best deal," and a romantic ideal of one perfect fit out there, the inevitable realization that the person you are with is not, in fact, perfect can be unsettling. And we are all imperfect people.

Over time, I passed through this phase. My wife is amazing in a million different ways, don't get me wrong, but what finally cured me from wondering whether there was someone else out there was the realization that perfection wasn't an attribute, but a result of a process. Once I figured out that what made my wife the perfect wife for me was not any or all of her many beautiful characteristics, but the commitment we made to each other and the way that commitment, and our life together, formed us to each other, I was able to bury that idol of liberty.

The next idol was that of possessiveness. Again, being relatively romantically inexperienced was probably a factor here. My wife has combated workaholic tendencies throughout her career, and especially as she was just getting started, it was really easy for her to have trouble leaving the office. Moreover, when she did get home, she'd often be exhausted, which made it challenging to kindle the flames of desire.

In my immaturity, I often wondered whether I had lost her affection. I worried that she might have found someone else more attractive and that she might be having an affair. Rationally, I knew that her exhaustion was real and work-related; even as an immature groom, I knew her character well enough not to doubt the sincerity of her fidelity to me. But deep down, a voice whispered otherwise, and even though my rival for my wife's time and attention wasn't another lover but her work, sometimes I wasn't as sure as I should have been.

Either way, the idol I had to defeat was possessiveness. As an immature lover, I clambered for the security of owning my wife completely. I know that there are many visions of marriage that hold this up as a real model for marital life, and I'm happy to say that I never really wanted or expected a barefoot and pregnant servant as a bride. But I can't say that I didn't want my wife's life to revolve around me first and foremost.

To a degree, that idol got pushed off the altar as I grew in actual love of my wife. To a larger degree, as I grew to appreciate her love for God and I came to share that same devotion, it was easier to let go of the idol of a me-centered marriage universe. With time, that idol has disappeared.

The marital idol that remains is the one illustrated in the parable Rolheiser tells above. Because the reality is, I love my wife, and being married to her, more than I can imagine loving anything else.

I've been aware of this for quite some time. The idea of "putting God first" isn't new to me, nor have I disagreed with its wisdom. But even now, I can't honestly say that I would rather have heaven than my wife. Whenever the reading comes up about the Sadducees grilling Jesus over who a woman who was married seven times would be married to in heaven, and Jesus responds that in heaven there is no marriage, I balk. Marriage is the absolutely best part of this life, in my experience. The idea of a heaven without it doesn't sound like heaven.

I recognize that, like Crete for the man in the parable, my wife is an idol that might stop me at heaven's gate. My only comfort is knowing that only the very best things in life can stay on the idol's perch that long and that powerfully.

Poor Paul.

This was my thought, briefly, when I realized at the start of Mass what I thought was about to happen.

Once every three years, the Church's liturgical cycle of readings cues up a complete turkey of a reading that I have seldom heard acknowledged, much less preached on, from the pulpit. In I Corinthians 7:32-35, St. Paul lays out an argument about marriage that sounds like (and probably was) a knock on married life:

> *Brothers and sisters: I should like you to be free of anxieties. An unmarried man is anxious about the things of the Lord, how he may please the Lord. But a married man is anxious about the things of the world, how he may please his wife, and he is divided. An unmarried woman or a virgin is anxious about the things of the Lord, so that she may be holy in both body and spirit. A married woman, on the other hand, is anxious about the things of the world, how she may please her husband. I am telling you this for your own benefit, not to impose a restraint upon you, but for the sake of propriety and adherence to the Lord without distraction.*

Poor Paul, I thought. Not St. Paul, but Paul, our church's brand-new permanent deacon. For those who aren't familiar, since the mid-1960s, Roman Catholicism has revived the role of permanent deacons, a form of ordination of married men for service to the Church that traces its roots back to the beginning of the Acts of the Apostles. And while deacons (then and now) are primarily called to serve the community in some unique way, they also (then and now) are allowed to preach at Mass. It's not really their main role, but it's a big deal, and for many of us it's the only encounter we have with deacons.

I had heard Deacon Paul preach once, and I have confidence in his ability to proclaim the Good News, but as I saw him on the altar with our associate pastor and heard this reading, I thought, "Oh no. I can totally see the priests looking at this reading, looking at their deacon, and saying, 'Why don't you take this one?'"

Proving again the mercy of our local priests, the associate took the homily and focused on the other readings. But even so, and even though I literally took a class on Corinthians from a professor who wrote one of the definitive commentaries on this, I heard three new things this Sunday in the midst of wondering whether Deacon Paul was going to have to make lemonade out of this.

First, St. Paul fails at his goal. He leads off this section by saying that he's providing this advice because he wants his listeners to be "free of all anxieties." Then he outlines how each of the states he considers, men and women, married and unmarried, *are all anxious*, just about different things. While there is a lot to say about the mindset from which Paul writes (which maybe we'll talk about another time), at the end of the day, Paul's advice doesn't help anyone be "free of all anxieties." Anxieties are a part of the human condition.

Second, when I go back and read what Paul says people are anxious about in these different states, I think "I wish!" He says those who aren't married are anxious about how to please God, and people who are married are anxious about how to please each other.

Would that it were so. In real life, we are all anxious about many things, and they usually aren't this noble. We're anxious about the bills and the promotion and the drama at the office or in the family and who's going to win the game on Sunday or the election on Tuesday. Lots and lots of things, none of them what Paul points to. Which is too bad.

And that's the third point. What Paul does point to as the sources of our anxiety — to please God and to please each other — are actually two paths to holiness. I know it's easier to see how Paul's vision of celibacy — as a freedom from attachment in order to directly pursue the divine — is a fast track to holiness. But as much as we may be culturally programmed to think that marriage is about other things, it is really a pathway to holiness every bit as powerful.

Think of it this way: when Jesus is asked what the Greatest Commandment is, he replies with a two-part answer: love God, love your neighbor. They both count. And while every neighbor is an opportunity to practice that divine call to love in a way that shapes both you and them, no relationship has more potential to unflinchingly carve out all that is not love in you than marriage. If you are really committed, as Paul says, to pleasing each other, you will learn both what sacrifice and joy look like, and they will form you in holiness.

We should probably do a better job of articulating the sanctifying challenge of matrimony to folks on the front end. I know that I didn't realize the full implications of what I signed up for at the time, and I also know that I don't do enough to ensure that the engaged couples I meet know what they are about to commit to. Even so, having a partner in the pursuit of love is a whole lot better than going it alone.

St. Paul, famously, didn't see it that way, and this passage in I Corinthians is part of his argument that the celibacy he chose was the better way. I know that choice has worked out well for many, and I guess it worked out OK for him, but still.

Poor Paul.

Projections

I have a daughter who is into projections. Which only makes sense.

She is currently in college, and she has discovered a passion for theatrical lighting design (and fireworks, but for the sake of the grandparents, we don't talk much about her interest in explosives as much). A lot of this stems from the fact that she grew up going to the theme parks that are not too far from us. We as a family were never that into the thrill rides, but we always closed the night with the fireworks extravaganzas that serve as the "kiss good night," and as the technology has developed, these have relied less and less on ordnance and more and more on computer-mapped video projections on castles, trees, globes and other buildings. These projections can take a thing (like a fiberglass castle), and make it appear to be a completely different thing (like a rocket actually launching from the ground). It is a remarkable technology.

And a relevant metaphor for me as a parent. When we first found out that we would be welcoming a child, I fairly quickly developed visions of what that child would be. If a boy, I imagined a football prodigy with a catchy nickname. If a girl, I imagined a feisty volleyball player, a fierce leader in pigtails.

Well, I got the pigtails, anyway.

When she was born, I used to joke that, as the child of an academic and a pseudo-academic, I was pretty sure that she would grow up to become a professional wrestler or else work for a traveling carnival, figuring that she would push back on all the book-learning in her heritage.

I turned out to be wrong about that one, too. She was a voracious reader from early on and is much smarter than her parents. Even if she *has* worked for a circus or two.

My point is, one of the real temptations of being a parent is projecting onto your kid what *you think* they should be and do and how you think they should live in the world. Sometimes, that looks like wanting your kid to do things just the way you do. Sometimes, it looks like wanting them to avoid the mistakes that you made. Either way, the sneaky idolatry I've seen in my own parenting life is wanting to make my child after my own image, rather than letting them be themselves.

It is an ongoing temptation to think that I always know best, and to think that somehow twisting this unique person into something that is less authentically them and more a projection of my expectations, hopes and fears, will work out well. It's no doubt rooted in putting myself at the center of my universe and expecting everyone else to coordinate their orbits around me. Which, at its foundation, is the idolatry of assuming that I'm the real Creator God around here.

Fortunately, my kid has been patient with me, and I've been quick enough to realize how much I am seam-burstingly proud of the person she is becoming. I would never have expected that she would pursue the paths that she has, but I have been so immensely proud of the way she has done so.

I never expected that she would want to pursue a career focused on the magic of projections, but I'm so glad that she's helping me grow out of the temptation to cast projections onto her.

Boxes

We put people in boxes in our mind. Maybe we do it so we can keep track of them, to keep all the people we know organized somehow. I don't know.

Sometimes we put them in boxes based on how we first met them. Sometimes we put them in boxes based on their worst choices. Sometimes we put them in boxes based on how they differ from us. Regardless, when we keep people in boxes, we miss a lot of their beauty, a lot of who they really are. We need to learn to let them out so we can appreciate the whole of them.

A lot of people on my team started their career with our organization in one role, but have grown in responsibility or changed streams or otherwise do something now that's different from when they started. And in that process, they have to, at some point, remind the people they work with, and a lot of times remind themselves, that they aren't in the same role as before.

This is a huge issue for parents, of course, who think of their 40-something multiple-degree-holding accomplished children as the same kid who didn't know how to tie his or her shoes and who ate anything they could pick up off the ground. But it's true for me, too; about one-third of my team at work interned with us at some point, and not only do I not appreciate who they were *before* they walked into my life, but I also tend to remember them as interns long after they have outgrown that role. I have to let them out of that box.

Sometimes we put people in a box based on how they differ from us. I'm thinking of a person I used to work with who really liked the spotlight. We are all the heroes of our own personal story, I think, but her story seemed more dramatic in the telling than others, and I am someone who, despite initial appearances, dreads direct attention. I am allergic to compliments, for instance; I take them horribly and would rather not have the fuss. Because this person had a different style, I kept her in a "drama queen" box for a while, and if I didn't let her out, I would have missed the beauty of her soul. I would have forgotten how quick she was to help me when a family member was diagnosed with the same chronic illness she wore so gracefully. I would have overlooked how gentle and kind-hearted she was.

We put people in boxes to make them easier to understand, and when we do that, we can fail to understand them at all. We miss some of the best parts, we don't see their souls dance, because we trap them in a box. Maybe it makes us feel better to have the power to label someone and put them on an interior shelf, but the reality is, whatever satisfaction we gain from that feeble, false power is more than overcome by the loss of encounter of the full beauty of that other person.

So if we catch ourselves putting someone in a box today, let's be sure we let them out.

• • • •

Originally published February 2018

Pope Francis is not only right about dogs, he is prophetic.

Over the past few years, Pope Francis has made news on several occasions by scolding people who choose pet ownership over child-rearing. In recent remarks about the declining birth rate in Italy, the pope again chided those who elevate their dog to the status of a human child (though he has much more to say about the systemic issues driving the declining birth rate). And every time a comment like this comes out, it captures headlines and gets blowback from dog owners.

I am a dog owner, but I also believe he's right. More than that, I think the popular reaction to his comments illustrates the prophetic nature of his point.

First, a little context. While there is no papal dog, Pope Francis isn't against animals. He is, after all, named for Saint Francis of Assisi, tamer of the wolf of Gubbio, and perhaps his most significant encyclical to date, *Laudato Si*, introduces a commitment to the care of creation (including animals) to an elevated place in Catholic social teaching. Search the internet, and you will find many photos of the pope in the company of dogs without any tinge of antipathy.

When Pope Francis speaks to the decline in birth rates, he doesn't focus solely on the substitution of pets for children. He has spoken at length about the systemic factors undermining population growth (or even population maintenance), things like an economic system that requires couples to pursue dual careers and yet still does not provide financial security that allows home ownership, lack of support systems like affordable child care that make child-bearing economically daunting, and biases against mothers in the workforce that in many cultures require women to give up their careers in order to raise a child. It is not just about the dog strollers.

Yet Francis also contrasts the money spent on pets with the needs of children in poverty. When Americans in particular spend billions on pet care, including "doggie day care," "pet therapists," all sorts of clothing, and, yes, dog strollers, all while poverty continues to affect fellow humans here and around the globe, it is easy to see how the pope could see a disconnect. We are called to love our neighbor, but many a T-shirt proclaims that we prefer our pets. I know many journalists can tell stories of how exposés of human suffering bring little reader and viewer response, but a displaced or neglected animal brings scores of calls and letters offering to help. Not only do individuals and families choose pet ownership instead of children; our society cares more about pets than (other people's) kids.

A true prophet holds up God's reality to ours and shows us the gaps. This is what Francis has done in talking about our outsized elevation of pets. You can tell this by the forcefulness of the reaction to his statements.

One way to think about idolatry, about the transgression of the First Commandment, is to identify what we are unwilling to give up, if God asked. In effect, Francis' comments on pets offer the opportunity to test ourselves: if God asked us to give up our devotion to our dogs (or cats), would we be willing to? Can we keep our pets in their proper place in the hierarchy of loves, below God and neighbor?

Our answer, as shown by our passionate disapproval of Francis' comments, is that a lot of us can't. When confronted with the choice between God's call to holiness and our pets' call for devotion, Fifi and Fido win almost every time.

Look, I love dogs. I have many other areas of my life in which, given the choice between pursuing holiness and holding onto what I have, I'll stick with what I have. I am, as are we all, an idolator.

But that doesn't mean that the pope's not right about dogs. It just means I have work to do on myself, and maybe I'm not the only one.

Distraction

I was never a high priest in the temple. But I was definitely an acolyte. When does escape become an idol? When what happens in the world you only pretend to inhabit affects you more than what happens in the world you really live in.

When I was in graduate school studying what anthropologists and sociologists identified as common elements of religion and ritual, across cultures, times and belief systems, I kept thinking the same thought. *They aren't describing what happens on Sunday in church. They're describing what happens on Saturday at college football games.*

I got my master of divinity degree with no intent of using it as an ordained minister. And by "no intent," I mean I joined the Roman Catholic Church, which forbids married priests (with some narrow exceptions), just before I graduated and two years after I got married.

I went on to do doctoral work focused on Christian political thought, which was housed within the religion department's program on Ethics and Society, which meant I needed to take sociology of religion courses as part of the process. That wasn't the course that cured me of any interest in a career in academia; in many ways, it's the course that most prepared me for life on the outside.

Big-time sports is a religion, albeit one without any claims on what is ultimately real. Your team (and mine) is a cult of belonging, with strictly prescribed uniforms and colors, chants and cheers and songs, prescribed group motions, and beliefs about good and evil that are all designed to direct the adherent toward becoming part of something bigger than themselves, whether that be Raider Nation or the Cameron Crazies or the Bronx Zoo.

My father-in-law was working on the Ohio State campus when I was in graduate school, and I was fortunate enough to be able to go to a Buckeyes home football game with him. Unfortunately, I didn't have a paper due around then. We wore scarlet and gray. We attended a "skull session" in the basketball arena, which was a combination of a pep rally and a warmup for the band. We entered the ultimate temple, the Horseshoe, to watch the entrance first of the band and then the team. We sang "Hang on Sloopy" and cheered along with the crowd until we were lost in the whole of them. Decades later, I have no idea who they played (though I know the Buckeyes won), but I remember the feeling of belonging to a tribe. That is what religious cults and their rituals do, in every culture and time.

The funny thing is, though, I don't recall ever being that tempted by the idol of sports tribalism. I'm sure that's because I rooted only for teams that were mediocre or worse, with uninspired fan bases. There was no cult for my high school football team, or the college basketball team that (seemingly) I alone grew up rooting for, or for my alma mater's teams (they only excelled in golf during my tenure). My professional teams have always been cellar-dwellers and startups. The Tampa Bay Devil Rays never had a skull session.

And yet sports provided me another idol.

When I was a kid, I always hoped I would make my way in sports. At first, I thought I could maybe make it as a relief pitcher; in the 1970s, athleticism didn't seem to be a prerequisite for that position. An arm was, though, so early on I realized that I would have a better shot as a basketball coach, or better yet, a Major League Baseball general manager.

I was part of the last generation that knew baseball cards as something fun, rather than as an investment choice. I had thousands of cards, which I played with daily, sorting out with each pack whether I could make a decent team from the players whose pictures were on the cards. The idea of being a decision-maker, of constructing a roster to win a championship, was really enticing. If I couldn't hit or pitch or catch a lick, I could dream about gathering the right mix of those who could.

If your heart is set on being a decision-maker like that, you realize that there are a lot of ways to pretend to play that role, but very few opportunities to do so in real life. Even before fantasy sports were a thing, I immersed myself in pretend scenarios for leading when the world I lived in didn't offer those kinds of chances. When my hometown, Jacksonville, won the right to an NFL expansion team, I spent hours, even days, evaluating the available players to be drafted from college or signed away from other teams. The real Jaguars did not ask my advice, but had they done so, I had answers, baby.

Years earlier, in college classes, I would doodle out the depth chart and draw up plays for the perennially hopeful basketball team at my school. Years later, I did the same thing when St. Petersburg was awarded the baseball team for which it had built its domed temple.

At this point in my life, I make enough real decisions to keep my mind occupied. And in fairness, I think the fantasy opportunities I created in my youth gave me practice and honed some skills that at least indirectly prepared me for these real choices.

But the cold, hard truth is, for a lot of my early years, I cared more about what happened in the sports world that was not my existence than I did in the reality in which I lived.

Maybe for some, the idol of escape isn't one about decision-making fantasy worlds. It could be that belonging is the idol — when sports fans lob death threats at athletes or poison the grounds of their opponents or bind themselves to rituals that they believe can will their team to victory, it looks a lot like they've given allegiance to an idol.

When fans care more about what happens on the field of play than what's going on in real life, that looks like an idol, too. As I write this, a governor and presidential candidate is threatening to sue over the exclusion of his college football team from the playoffs, a sentiment for which most of the state is supportive. What does it say that we can generate more energy in defense of a college football team's playoff hopes than we can for providing basic necessities for real people in our midst?

Maybe you're not a sports fan. Maybe your escape hatch is in literature, or movies, or theater, or popular culture. Maybe it's in politics, or reality television. The temples are everywhere to this idol that offers us a chance to escape reality for something more interesting. How many of us know which house at Hogwarts we would belong to, but not which neighbor is really struggling with depression?

I never got to be a coach or a general manager, much less a relief pitcher. The closest I got was selling tickets to the show, a money changer in the temple. Once I realized that that was as close as I was likely to get to the fantasy world of leading a team, I wandered away.

I'm still tempted by the idol of escape. I can get caught up in a TV show, or a project, to the point that I start to see the world through its eyes. But I've had to learn, over a long time, that the most attractive escape can still only deliver saccharine emptiness that satisfies less than even the bitter notes of living my mundane but real life.

Since I left a doctoral program in religion focused on society and ethics to go work in collegiate and professional sports for five years, after spending my seminary "supervised ministry" work as an intern with the Atlanta Braves' chaplain, the interplay between religion and sports has always been in the back of my mind.

Even though medical experts seem to think that what happened to Buffalo Bills player Damar Hamlin when he collapsed after a hit and his heart stopped on the field of play during a playoff game on January 2, 2023 was a freak injury – one that happens around 30 times a year, more often with Little League catchers than high-level football players – the shocking nature of this incident – the suddenness and visibility of a player collapsing in the middle of a nationally televised game – has magnified issues that were always there under the surface. The best and worst of the American phenomenon of big-time football (be it NFL or major college football) is all so brilliantly on display.

But "Does God like football?" is a hard question to ask, especially for those of us who like football ourselves.

Football is first and foremost a sport, which can be considered along with the performing arts as a sort of non-ultimate good. At their best, performance-based activities like these have direct and indirect benefits for both participants and spectators that are lesser versions of divine goods. Participants pursue excellence, commit themselves to discipline, develop self-sacrificial bonds of community, and, perhaps most uniquely, communicate a radiating sense of joy when they are able to perform their roles at the best of their ability, reflecting a sense of fulfilled vocation lived in the moment that is apparent for all to see. Spectators have the ability to witness and be inspired by that joy, while also learning to appreciate beauty, honor the excellence of others, and, especially in sports fan bases, develop community among fellow spectators.

These elements are good in that they cater to the best of human nature, and they are reflective of goods that we are called to in our ultimate vocation as spiritual beings. Pursuing and appreciating excellence, embracing discipline, sacrificing our desires for the good of the other, and developing community are all attitudes and skills that we are called to hone in our spiritual lives. For those who accept the notion of natural revelation, through which we can come to know something of God through the function of the world, it is easy to see how sports like football might offer breadcrumbs of experience that prepare us for the pursuit of more meaningful versions of the same goods.

Even in the Hamlin case, we see the elements of potential holiness. Players from both teams, those in the stadium, and millions around the country, prayed actively and fervently together. Even in subsequent days, commentators on sports shows prayed openly, something generally considered taboo in secular culture. Hundreds of thousands of fans donated millions of dollars to Hamlin's charity, which had previously raised only a few thousand dollars, as a sign of compassion. Surely those instincts – to suffer with, to pray for, to support a fellow human being beset by tragedy – are ones that connect directly to our vocation as spiritual beings. Yes, there are thousands if not millions of people in the world whose need should engender this sort of response. But at least we responded to this one. That's a start we can build on, right?

Sports also have some more morally ambiguous elements. Foremost is the nature of sports as competitive, pitting individuals and teams against each other. On the one hand, this zero-sum element of sports fosters and feeds division, which is contrary to God's original plan and ongoing will for humanity as a unified family. On the other hand, team sports like football require the development of strong bonds of self-sacrifice that, in our fallen nature, are often best created in the face of an opponent. While we are ultimately called to see that we all belong to each other, sports can play an intermediary role of calling us out beyond our own selfishness to recognize that we belong to, if not everyone, at least those on our team. This argument is similar to the theological justification of nations. It is an imperfect good, perhaps justified by whether it prepares us for or impedes us from the perfect good of unity.

Likewise ambiguous is the similarity between culturally significant sporting events and religious ritual. Through the symbols of colors, clothing, chants and cheers, and prescribed forms of behavior, the crowd at a sporting event replicates many of the elements of religious ritual. In the experience of losing themselves to the larger whole of the crowd, fans can experience something akin to spiritual transcendence. (I have argued that college and pro football games are often more textbook religious rituals, and more consistent gateways to this form of transcendental experience, than most church services.) Whether these experiences prepare and inspire us to pursue similar transcendent experiences that connect us to the divine, rather than just to our football team, is unclear.

Then there are the more challenging moral questions. Much of the current discussion revolves around the degree to which football in particular jeopardizes the health and well-being of participants, as well as the degree to which this specific sport glorifies violence. Though what happened to Damar Hamlin may well have been a freak occurrence, in the 21st century there has been much greater scrutiny of the long-term impact of football on the health of former players. Most of that attention has been on brain health and CTE, though in reality the wear-and-tear of playing football appears to have an outsized effect on lots of other body parts. One can argue that every sport and even some performing arts include levels of this sort of physical risk. In some cases, the common awareness of physical risks accentuates the more transcendent components of the experience for both participant and spectator (I think of circus artists as an example). But it is hard to argue that God wants us to risk our lives for a sport, which has no intrinsic value.

Football in particular has a history and design that glorifies violence. While the 21st century implementation of brain-safety protocols seeks to protect participants, there remains a significant part of the game that celebrates "big hits." It is no accident that football players frequently use metaphors of war in describing their pursuit, and some social theorists have identified sports like football as evolutionary replacements for war as outlets for aggression. But (for non-pacifists) war can be justified under specific criteria. Violence in the pursuit of protecting others, for instance, may sometimes be seen as virtuous. The violence of football, though, does not occur within that larger moral context.

More damning is the role that culturally central sports play within systems and structures that violate the dignity of every human being. A common critique of capitalism is that the systems in place can promote "profits over people," ignoring the essential human dignity of every participant in favor of the economic success of the venture. Many of the critiques of those who called for the Bills-Bengals game to be resumed focused on this. Not only might resumption of play dishonor the dignity of Hamlin, who at that point was fighting for his life, but it also would have ignored the impact of witnessing the potential death of a fellow player on the mental state of both teams' players. Though a more humane response carried the day, the fact that this was a debate at all highlights the temptation to reduce players to commodities in a sport that has such direct and indirect economic consequences.

But ultimately, the problem with football is bigger than all of this. Because the reality is, many of us don't want a God who doesn't like football. Wags have pointed out that NFL attendance has rebounded much more quickly and fully than has church attendance since the pandemic-related lockdowns. As I mentioned earlier, people commit hours of time to participating as a spectator in a football ritual, painting faces and wearing jerseys, tailgating with traditional food and drink and cheering through a 3+ hour game filled with blaring music and rituals that might seem quirky to outsiders. Far fewer people are as committed to church rituals.

Since the beginning of our existence, humanity has had an idolatry problem. The evidence is pretty clear that for many of us, football is today's idol. Unless we are willing to give it up, it's pretty easy to know whether God likes football.

Even if football may be an idol for a lot of us, Christians could learn a thing or two from the sport. Encountering God is a lot more like a football game than a book group.

One of the things that I struggle with is the degree to which many Christians talk about their faith in dispassionate, philosophical terms. In Catholicism, there's a tendency to elevate the Ancient Greek philosophers to such a degree that I sometimes wonder if there's a "St. Epictetus" or "St. Aristotle" statue hiding in the Vatican somewhere. Among mainline Protestants, the devotion to the Greeks may not be as strong, but there's often a post-Enlightenment approach to religious experience that can work so hard to show that faith and reason aren't opposites that it can intellectualize the emotion right out of the encounter with divinity. While the voices of faith that come either from beyond Western Europe, from its marginalized communities, or from more charismatic traditions may not suffer the same desiccation, many Christian circles in the dominant culture sound a lot more like book groups than fan zones. One Sunday's Bible verses speak to a different side of faith.

Listen to Jeremiah 20:7-9

> *You duped me, O LORD, and I let myself be duped;*
> *You were too strong for me, and you triumphed...*
> *I say to myself, I will not mention him, I will speak in his name*
> *no more.*
> *But then it becomes like fire burning in my heart, imprisoned*
> *in my bones;*
> *I grow weary holding it in, I cannot endure it.*

Or Psalm 63

My soul is thirsting for you, O Lord my God....

For you my flesh pines and my soul thirsts like the earth, parched, lifeless and without water....

You are my help, and in the shadow of your wings I sing for joy.

My soul clings fast to you; your right hand upholds me.

Or Romans 12:1-2 (one of my favorites)

I urge you, brothers and sisters, by the mercies of God, to offer your bodies as a living sacrifice...

Or Matthew 16, where Jesus predicts his Passion, Peter tells him "ix-nay on the uffering-say," and Jesus compares him to Satan, before explaining:

Whoever wishes to come after me must deny himself, take up his cross, and follow me. For whoever wishes to save his life will lose it, but whoever loses his life for my sake will find it.

I have been guilty of reading through these while going through the motions, without reflecting on the passion in each of them. I don't think I'm alone in this. There is a setting of Psalm 62 that somehow turns "My soul is thirsting for you O Lord" into a harmless little ditty you can kind of hum along to. If you know it, it is probably stuck in your head right now. Sorry.

No, really. I *am* sorry. Because the words of the Psalmist and of Jeremiah and Paul and Matthew's Jesus, when you really notice them, don't lend themselves to pleasant settings. They speak to a level of emotion, a level of passion, that belongs to genres other than hymns – driving beats or fierce instrumentals or raw vocals.

My point is not to critique music, though. It's to ask whether by silencing the longing, hunger and thirst of those who have encountered God directly and are willing to sacrifice themselves totally as a result of that encounter, we've buried the element of faith that speaks most directly to the human heart.

It's week one of college football, and the NFL kicks off next week. I let myself be duped, too... when I think my team is better than it turns out to be. The fire burning in my heart usually has more to do with getting a defensive stop than anything holy. I don't offer my body as a living sacrifice, but I cheer for those who do (and I know some of y'all still will go at least as far as to apply some face paint before a game). That we are more passionate about our teams than we are about our God isn't football's fault. It's ours.

Every "Yes" is a "No"

This is my new mantra, apparently. I know it's not original to me and I suspect I read it somewhere years ago. But about four months ago, "Every yes is a no" popped out of my mouth during a work discussion, and now it keeps coming to mind in all sorts of settings. Mainly because it pulls back the curtain of the hidden consequences of our decisions.

When you say yes to a project that takes your time, you will say no to other demands on your time, whether you acknowledge those nos or not.

When you say yes to something that costs a dollar, that becomes a dollar you can't spend elsewhere.

When you say yes to a relationship by giving it your attention (which is at the heart of love), you are saying no to other relationships.

Usually, following the standard rule of improv comedy, we think we can say yes without saying no. We are a culture of "yes, and..." as the improv folks say. It doesn't really work that way, though. When we say yes, but then add an "and," we ignore the fact that cutting an extra slice of a pie only comes at a cost to the other slices. If we keep adding luggage to the plane, it will eventually not be able to fly.

Most of these yeses and nos are partial. We don't usually put all our chips in the center of the table; even in our biggest decisions, we are usually only establishing a main priority and claiming how much of our limited resources will go into the innermost of the concentric circles of our priorities.

Many of these yeses and nos can be for a limited time. I invest a dollar now, saying no to other ways of spending it today, in hopes of having two dollars to spend at some time in the future. I take an hour away from friends and family to rest and replenish so that the hours I spend with them later will be more vibrant and meaningful. We do this all the time, and sometimes the deferred gratification pays off.

Sometimes it doesn't, because the investment doesn't gain back interest, or the future time never materializes.

Those who we hold up as great — the star athletes and titans of business and master artists and performers and saints — usually share a rare ability to hold strong on their commitment to the yes at the center of their circle. That one thing, whatever it is, is a commitment they prioritize so highly that they successfully push off the chorus of "ands." (That sometimes means that in other areas of their lives, they are horrible failures.) Regardless, they serve as the counterpoint to the rest of us, who let the "ands" creep in. Without acknowledging the opportunity costs, we diminish our ability to excel at what we say is our top priority.

I have wanted to say that somehow love short-circuits this calculus, but I don't think it does. Instead, I think love reveals the flip side of this "Every yes is a no" mantra. As much as the yes/no framework implies that ultimately, everything is a choice we make as independent actors, the truth is, every choice shapes us in return. When I say yes to the ruthless pursuit of excellence, I become more ruthless. When I say yes to the pursuit of wealth, I become more bound by greed. When I say yes to an ascetic rejection of the world, I become more quick to reject what's around me.

There is no hack to "every yes is a no." There is only the promise that comes with choosing the right thing to say *yes* to, the thing we prioritize enough to let it shape us.

Noted fictional philosopher, gambler and theologian Danny Ocean once said, "The house always wins. Play long enough, you never change the stakes, the house takes you. Unless, when that perfect hand comes along, you bet big, and then you take the house."

There is only one perfect hand. Love for the Ultimate Love. If we say yes to Love in a big enough way that we go all in, and we maintain the primacy of that yes in the face of other opportunities to whittle off little pieces of attention for lesser yesses, with the unwavering commitment of a Michael Jordan, a sneaky transformation happens. If we love the right "other" fully enough, the act of loving changes us. With the practice of committing time and attention to our beloved, we find ourselves more loving to others. To give away the magician's trick here, our hearts aren't actually growing, no matter what the Grinch says. Instead, love is the act of putting a beloved's interest ahead of your own; as we practice it more committedly, we shrink how much of our heart, time and attention we reserve for ourselves. Over time, the love we held back for ourselves when we thought we went "all-in" becomes available to us to offer to others. That is how love begets love.

The trick is to find a beloved worthy enough to devote that much of your heart to, one that won't exploit your gift but will allow your act of giving to ennoble you. Then it's just a matter of staying disciplined.

There is only one Beloved worthy of that big a yes. It's not a lover or a child or a spouse, but the divine Lover who is Love.

Every yes is a no. But if you say yes in a big enough way to a beloved worthy of the scale of it, and keep that yes from being "and-ed" down, you take the house.

I've noticed that the theme of a lot of current health trends is to stay in the moment.

The key to strength training, I'm told, is to be intentional about each moment of each rep of weights; rather than seeing how many times you can lift something or how heavy a thing you can lift, maintaining an intentional effort throughout the process – focusing on keeping your muscles tense from the moment the weight lifts off the ground through the moment you put it back down – is the key.

The same goes for cardio, where high intensity interval training emphasizes not the amount of time you're moving, but how intensely you keep your focus in that time of movement.

I haven't read this anywhere, but I know personally that if, theoretically, I paid attention to every bite of food I ate, rather than shoveling in whatever was in front of me while I read/watched/listened to something else, I'd do a much better job of attending to what my body needed and be healthier as a result.

So it is with relationships. It's great to spend a whole day in the company of someone you love, for sure. But it's entirely different to spend time focused on each other rather than simply coexisting, side by side. And conversely, the easiest way I have found to devalue time with someone important to you is to be focused on something else when they have something to tell you. Damn you, internet!

Why is it so hard to stay in the moment, to be in the place your feet are?

Philosophers and theologians have debated for centuries what it is that separates us from other animals, and Reinhold Niebuhr has the best argument, for my money. Alone among the animals, he argues, we humans have the ability to see beyond ourselves, to take in the big picture, to look over the horizon. But along with that gift comes the weight of knowing our own limits. I can look back on a time before I existed, and I can look ahead to the time when I will no longer exist. And that makes me anxious. I am running out of time.

It's the paradox of who we are that, driven by the fear of running out of time, we spend the time we have someplace other than the present moment. The more we dwell in the past or fret about the future, the less attention we pay to now, whether that now is doing something mundane (like eating or exercising or trying to sleep) or something transcendent like spending time with another. Much more so spending time with the ultimate Other; I have the grocery lists made in alleged prayer time to prove it.

Jesus covered this, you know. At the end of Matthew 6, in the section known as the Sermon on the Mount that is often considered the Cliff's Notes of Jesus' message, he says, "Therefore do not worry about tomorrow, for tomorrow will worry about itself. Each day has enough trouble of its own." (6:34, NIV translation) I'll admit I prefer the dark poetry of the NAB translation of that line: "Sufficient for a day is its own evil."

Fr. Greg Boyle of Homeboy Industries (one of my heroes) is the first person I saw turn "Now hear this" into "Now. Here. This." in an effort to focus on the present. But some days, honestly, the best I can do is bracket off the past and future with "Sufficient for a day…"

Take the Big Trip

Leisure is not the privilege of those who have time, but rather the virtue of those who give to each instant of life the time it deserves. — Br. David Steindl-Rast

"Take the big trip."

I was catching up with a good friend who said this, not as a directive, but as a descriptor of a moment she was going through with her circle. She rattled off several friends of hers who had either lost a spouse or been diagnosed with cancer at way too young an age, and captured the impact of that mini-trend as one of those "take the big trip" reminder moments. Because tomorrow is not promised.

I have been in a "Take the big trip" moment lately, too. We are at the age, perhaps, when life hits this point hard. In our 50s, we still have kids on the payroll and a significant stretch of years until retirement, so time chugs along on the routine of a daily/monthly/yearly grind of banal normalcy. But, like it or not, we find out that we are old enough for our cohort to be handed a share of brutal diagnoses that is a lot larger than the rare and tragic losses we felt in our 20s and 30s. Where before, we might have been lulled into believing that tomorrow was at least a pretty safe bet, that illusion is wearing away now.

One of the sad-but-instructive lessons of working with a lot of retirees is that, earlier than many, I knew people who had learned the hard way that tomorrow is not promised.

I especially remember a couple who volunteered with us as early retirees. That had not been their plan. They expected to have years, maybe decades, to travel the world once they retired, but the oncologists revealed a different future to them. They were wonderful people, great volunteers, and relentlessly upbeat, which in hindsight is really remarkable, because I would have been pissed had I been in their shoes. They had postponed so many of their dreams for a day that, as it turns out, not only had never been promised but would not ever come. That they moved forward with a sense of joy in a different direction than the one they wanted is a testament to their character and a sign of hope for the rest of us.

I was surprised by the people I knew who were nudged by the pandemic to retire earlier than they might have been planning. I sure don't blame them, though, since the whole society was reckoning with the reality that tomorrow is not promised.

There are, I think, two idols that I struggle to let go of here.

The first is maybe more obvious: the illusion that my future is somehow truly mine to map out and control. Despite the many lessons to the contrary, I still find myself thinking through "the plan" that writes an advance story on how the next four decades will roll out. Even during my "take the big trip" moments, I tend to respond like a slow quarterback who sees the defensive pressure coming; I may speed up my process a bit, but I keep working through my progression of decision points, rather than ditching the plan and scrambling to make the most of the moment. I do not need any more evidence that time is not mine to control, but that doesn't keep me from forecasting my retirement security index.

And that presumption, that in the end, I am in charge, is certainly a false god.

But there is another idol here, too.

How do you spend the time you're given?

I *don't* spend a lot of the time I'm given. I just *waste* it. How much of my day is oriented neither toward a worthwhile pursuit nor toward truly enjoying the moment I am in? How many hours aren't in any way connected to loving God or anyone else, myself included? The "screen time" report on my phone is an opening data point in the indictment. Even in the face of lives cut too short, I find myself wasting time, not in restorative, leisurely appreciation, but in the pretend busyness of our age. Scrolling to the end of a social media feed. Following every link of every emailed newsletter. Playing one more game of Sudoku. That I can both know how precious and unpromised life is and yet still squander it is a sure sign of desperate addiction.

Tomorrow is not promised. That this isn't a new or profound revelation, and yet it remains unable to persuade me to "give to each instant of life the time it deserves," speaks to the power of the idol.

Repurposing Those Abandoned Temples

Let's go back to the White House and Mar-a-Lago. (Or let's not).
Why did I feel like I was revisiting temples where I had once worshiped but since abandoned during that three-week stretch of visits to the upper echelons of American politics? To answer that question, let's take a step back and reflect on the different idols I've found the need to give up on.

Maybe one of the foundational elements of faith is the assertion that "God is God, and I am not." While that simple phrase can take a lifetime to truly accept as a liberating truth rather than an insult, to the extent that we do, we are called to raze the temples whose idols are really just mirrors of ourselves.

Pride — that I matter more — is such an idol. So is control — that I am or need to be in charge. We can talk about the need for basic self-respect and the adage of "pray like everything depends on God, act like everything depends on you," as less idolatrous expressions of pride and control, but, at least for me, I've learned that both pride and control are drugs that are hard to quit and impossible to take in limited doses. I would argue that my goal is to raze the temples to pride and control.

Relationships and purpose, on the other hand, are clearly temples that require reconsecration. God is essentially Love, which centers relationship at the core of the spiritual life. Marriage, family, friendship, the loose ties of sharing community with acquaintances — all of these relationships fit within holiness, when they reserve room for relationship with God at the head of the table.

Likewise, my long search for purpose didn't end with the realization that we are essentially purposeless. Far from it! We *are* made for a purpose, and the journey of my young adulthood was one of recognizing that, whatever vocations and projects I am called to, they only provide purpose within the context of a primary "Yes" to purpose through relationship with the divine.

Honestly, I'm still not sure what to do with distraction. Some distractions, I have tried to reconsecrate, like using social media to little-e evangelize. Other distractions, I have had to eliminate, because there is no holy purpose to them. And some, maybe, I can learn to repurpose into something that may not be holy per se, but fills a healthy role in a life. I'm still working on figuring that out.

What was I confronting within myself at Mar-a-Lago and the White House? Politics today is about nothing if not about pride and power (or control). Our culture's bitter partisanship has bred toxic relationships rooted in "us-them" thinking. For many, politics has supplanted God as their ultimate purpose. For many more, it has become one of the most addicting of distractions. I have many friends who keep a TV on cable news all day while being serenaded by pings of alert notifications, all focused on the politics that centers around what happens at places like the White House and Mar-a-Lago.

All the idols I have been convinced to quit, all wrapped up in two big houses.

I'd like to say that we can build a politics around dialogue toward the common good rather than wrestling over control of levers of power. I'd like to say that we can reintroduce humility and healthy, respectful relationships in political discourse.

But for me, for now, all I know is that the temples of today are still filled with idols I need to stay away from. They say that newly recovering alcoholics are no fun at parties. Maybe my reaction during those three weeks was an acknowledgment that, in this case, the same could have been said of me.

Toward a Non-Idolatrous Politics

At our core, we don't have a political problem. We have an idolatry problem.

In the wake of the shooting of former President and Republican presidential candidate Donald Trump, there have been many new calls to return civility to politics. Before we can hope to regain civility, much less the focus on the common good, though, we need to first address the theological elephant in the room: American politics, for too many, is idolatrous. Unless we can dethrone the idol of politics and return it to a place of subordinate value, civility and the common good will remain elusive.

How do we know that American politics has crossed the line into idolatry? First, for many, political allegiance is our primary source of identity and holds a primary claim on our time and attention. It is one thing to be an informed citizen, but quite another to spend hours on end watching politically biased news commentary, listening to podcasts and talk radio, and otherwise surrounding yourself with political messaging that reinforces a worldview. Perhaps we all would benefit from a simple examination of conscience: is our devotion of time and attention to politics greater than that to God, or even to family?

Second, we see the true expression of religious faith alloyed by political allegiance. Much has been made of the allegiance of many Catholic, evangelical and protestant churches - both pastoral leaders and congregations - with the American populist movement. To a lesser degree, the same temptation to political alignment appears in congregations on the American left. While faith can and must inform our positions on issues affecting the common good, when we are tempted to assume that "God's way" aligns perfectly with "my way" or "my party's way," we are clearly off track. A simple application of Catholic social teaching makes clear that Catholics cannot be fully comfortable with either party's platform.

Third, even among Christians, theological virtues are overcome by the political culture of fear. We follow a Christ who desired our unity, but we allow political allegiances to divide us. We proclaim a gospel of hope, but we live in a constant state of political dread that, if our opponent wins, all will be lost. We worship a God who desires our unity, but we live in a political culture that depends on fear to maintain divisive tribal loyalties.

It is possible to participate in the political process without making it an idol. For almost 25 years, I have worked as a policy advocate at the national, state and local levels for a (secular) non-partisan organization, which has given me an immersive view of the political process and lots of practice at working to achieve good policy in contentious debates. Here are three suggestions from my experience.

First, we are "members" of many things, from the Body of Christ to families of origin to fan or hobby clubs to loyalty rewards programs at our local coffee shop. Some of those memberships define us, and some are just a way to engage more efficiently with the world. Don't let your political party membership creep above family and faith in defining you.

Second, stay uncomfortable with your faith. The Gospel is meant both to console and challenge us; when I am comfortable enough to feel a tinge of triumphalism about my faith and its application to my political views, I know I've developed a blind spot to the gaps that remain between our temporal structures and eternal truths.

And third, choose love, not fear. When I am tempted to demonize an opponent, I know I've fallen for fear. I can counter that by remembering that God's love extends to all of us, and I am challenged to mirror that divine reality in how I treat the people I disagree with. When I'm tempted to despair about our future, I know I've forgotten the God whose world this is.

Until we fix our idolatry problem, we'll never fix our politics.

Be(4) - A Going-away Message to My daughter

Be Here.
Be Grateful.
Be Generous.
Be Bold.

· · · ·

Be Here. We miss so much by not really being present to the moment. We don't notice beauty. We skip opportunities to love. We don't tap into joy. All because we're not really here, wherever here is, because we're caught up thinking about something that happened before or looking ahead to something that might come ahead or else lost in a virtual world that isn't really here. The richness in life is here.

Be Grateful. The guys who started Life Is Good say two of the most powerful words in the English language are "Get to." How we approach things shapes our success and happiness. Over the last year and a half, there have been plenty of reasons to be disappointed, and I'm not saying you should pretend not to hurt when you hurt. But even amid the hurt, there are things to be grateful for. Even when we have hard things to do, we can focus on all the ways that we don't just "have to" do them, but we "get to" do them. Gratitude will shape the way you see life in ways that open you up to joy and love you'll miss otherwise. Be grateful.

Be Generous. It's no secret that I'm a big believer that love is what life is all about. But love is not just about the big loves — like family — but little loves to the people who come through your life briefly. And the threshold of living for love is to be generous. Don't do things because you're supposed to do them or because they're expected or they're the rules. Do things to be generous to the people around you.

Clean up your messes and a little bit of someone else's. Let the other person go first. When you notice something positive about someone, whether you like them or not, tell them. If you can make generosity your habit, you'll have to push yourself to do just a little bit more, but you'll find it's a more fulfilling way to live. Be generous.

Be Bold. Adults in general, and parents especially, focus on teaching kids to make safe choices. About driving, drinking, drugs, sex, walking through alleys late at night, all that. We forget to say that making safe choices really is important, but as a floor, not a ceiling. To really live requires making bold choices, too; choices to be all in, to be wholehearted, to go for your dreams. I have made bold choices that broke my heart. I have made bold choices that didn't work out. I have made bold choices that worked out differently than I thought. I have made bold choices that paid off. But the only choices I regret are the ones I made when I wasn't bold enough to put myself out there, when I was afraid to be vulnerable. I don't regret the heartbreaks; I regret the times I wasn't bold enough to risk my heart. Be bold.

· · · ·

Originally written to my daughter May 2021

The World is Our Cafe

Why should you read this book? This is less of a rhetorical question than it sounds, and I hope you'll let me know if you figure out a good answer. But let me offer that my purpose in sharing this is to tell a bit of my story in hopes that you might share some of yours in return.

The longer I live, the more certain I become that one of the most important and holiest things we can do is to know others and be known in return. A lot has been written about the epidemic of isolation and loneliness in our society. Here's my contribution.

When our daughter was working a couple hours away, we would go visit her frequently, and we got to know the area around her apartment complex pretty well. We used to have breakfast (and sometimes lunch) at a coffee shop right next to her place, and most of the time, the place was full of customers who came from her complex, college-age kids who worked where she did. It was crowded, but almost palpably lonely. Each person sat at their own table, staring at their phone, in silence. Very rarely, they might be talking with someone on video chat, but mostly, they were just scrolling alone.

I've seen this phenomenon in other places, but I think the fact that these were all 20-somethings at the start of their lives affected me more powerfully. I have worked in places where, at lunchtime, the parking lot is full of people eating lunch alone in their cars, but as sad as that makes me, I can understand as a fellow introvert that, if you work in a busy office, having a designated time out to recharge is a really valuable thing.

There's something much more poignant to me about sitting alone in a public place. Maybe the dynamic is the same — that the kids' apartments are crowded by extroverts and their work was in customer-facing roles that were a draining barrage of people — but something about spending time alone in a public cafe that is designed for conversation just feels sad.

During that season, I thought, maybe someday I would start a practice, a ministry, of showing up at a cafe like that with a sign that says something like "What's going on?" and then sitting and waiting for anyone who wanted to have another human being to talk to. Though I am an introvert who gets exhausted by big crowds and is useless at cocktail parties, there is something about one-on-one getting to know another person — their hopes, dreams, fears and daily grind — that feels like what we are here to do.

On reflection, this shapes how I go about my daily life in ways that make people really surprised to find out that I'm an introvert (as is my wife). Because we are creatures of routine, we go to the same places day after day, and we both have developed the habit of recognizing the people around us as protagonists of their own lives rather than just extras in ours. In very simple and basic ways, we express interest in the baristas and wait staff at our favorite places. I acknowledge to the people that I see at the pool that I notice when they are there and when they aren't. I look for ways to let people know they are seen, because it's easy in our world to feel invisible.

When I started posting reflections on Facebook many years ago, it opened a door that has led to some wonderful virtual examples of this sort of life-sharing. I don't think that's why I wrote them, per se, but sharing the thoughts that came to me with my Facebook friends in case they were helpful to anyone else has had the magical effect of enabling co-workers, former classmates, and other acquaintances to feel comfortable opening up about their lives.

Among the people who tell me they read my Facebook posts, the ones who mean the most are those who are on the periphery of faith. Many of them have given up on the Church (or believe the Church has given up on them), but my hope is that they haven't completely given up on God. My hope is that these posts of mine have offered a lifeline, if not to membership in a faith community, at least to the possibility that God is better than the worst of those who proclaim Him.

Recently, I started using an app to help me learn Italian that allows people to have 1:1 chats with mutual language learners. While the primary purpose is to offer feedback from a native English speaker to someone learning the language, while they correct my deficient Italian, the reality is that the content of those chats — how are you doing, what is your day like, what do you do, how's your family — often lead to deeper sharing about trials and joys in the here and now.

That made me realize something about the dream I had of a cafe ministry; it's not limited to a particular place or time or platform. The world is our cafe. Consider these pages my answer to your "What's going on?" sign. I look forward to hearing yours in return. Email me at AbandoningTemples@gmail.com.

Addendum: Ignite the Future

OK, let me introduce you to my friend Patrick.

Before I tell you the crazy story of how the Broadway musical *The Book of Mormon,* the Catholic Church, Bob Goff and Facebook converged to allow us to meet, and before I tell you how he presented some fundamental challenges to who I claim to be, you ought to meet him.

When I met Patrick, he lived in Nansana, a village in Wakiso, a region outside Kampala, in Uganda. He worked at Nansana Community Primary School, which cares for and educates and encourages kids whose parents can't take care of them or whose parents have died.

The recurring theme in talking about these kids is "their parents lost hope." Hope that they could get their kids an education. Hope that they could provide basic necessities. Hope that they could offer them a life. Nansana Community Primary School is the last hope for a bunch of kids in a poor area of a poor country that has been through a lot.

Patrick knows how important Nansana Community Primary School is because he sees what shape the kids are in when their parents drop them off. He hears their hopelessness. And he helps get the kids food, clothes, medical attention and an education.

But there's another reason Patrick knows the value of Nansana Community Primary School. Patrick was one of six kids with no father and a mother who did the best she could. Nansana was her last hope for Patrick, so she brought him there. When he graduated the primary and then the secondary school, he stayed around to help. As he told me:

> "Yes jeff thats my vision i every day request God to give me courage and help all kids that need help because i my self i was just helped,but if i wasnt helped i wouldnt have been what iam jeff"

So, it's kind of a crazy story, how I met Patrick.

I was in New York with my family for an epic Broadway trip, and the view out our hotel window was a church, St. Malachy's, that's known as the Actor's Chapel. On the streetlight in front of the Church is a banner for the Broadway play *The Book of Mormon,* which plays across the street from the church. My family and I liked the clean songs we heard from *The Book of Mormon,* enough to research the show before we went to New York. It turns out a lot of the songs are not so clean. It's a very profane send-up of the Mormon religion. And it's set in Uganda.

We joked that it is convenient that there's a church across from the theater, so you could go to Confession straight from seeing the show. We didn't, but we did go to Mass at St. Malachy's several times, including Sunday, June 3. That Sunday happened to be the Feast of Corpus Christi in the Catholic liturgical calendar, but normally June 3 is known as the day the church celebrates St. Charles Lawanga and companions. They are 19th century martyrs, the only ones I know that the Catholic Church honors from Uganda.

We were flying home on Monday the 4th and I was reading. I had two books, one of which was Bob Goff's *Everybody, Always.* I was reading a chapter a week. The other was a book I was trying to finish, but on the flight, something told me to finish *Everybody, Always,* which is a wonderful collection of funny and inspiring stories from Bob Goff's life in California. Until you get to the last five chapters or so, when it takes a turn to focus in depth on one gripping, challenging, deeply moving story. In Uganda.

So, I never thought about Uganda before, then all this.

So I posted something on Facebook:

> Here's my Uganda story from the weekend. Our hotel room overlooks St. Malachy's, which has a big *Book of Mormon*

street sign in front of it because the theater is across from the church. I find this funny. But then:

1) *The Book of Mormon* is set in Uganda.

2) The Saints of the day for the Sunday we were there were Charles Lawanga and companions, who were 19th century Ugandan martyrs.

3) On the plane ride home Monday, I decided not to read the book I really need to finish and read this other book instead. It's an awesome book, *Everybody, Always*, and you should read it. Almost all of it is a series of short, beautiful, inspirational and funny stories. But the last 3-4 chapters are different: an actual narrative about a really moving story. And guess where it's set?

God's gonna have to do more than that to get me to move to Uganda. But it's still kinda creepy.

I posted that late on June 5. On June 6, I got a Facebook friend request from someone in Uganda. Patrick. He'd just joined Facebook six weeks earlier to try to find people who could help the kids at his school. We had some mutual friends, so Facebook suggested me as a friend.

I know what you're thinking.

So, here's the deal. At that time in my social media life, I had made a strategic decision to be pretty open in my Facebook audience. When I get a friend request, I check three things:

1. Is it a front for a porn site or someone trying to get a date?
2. Is it someone solely pushing their business?
3. Is it someone who just focuses on politics?

If those are all no, I'll accept.

Patrick passed that test. But usually, if a new friend starts trying to engage me on Messenger, the deal is off. Were it not for the confluence of Uganda events, he would have lost me at "hello." But hard on the heels of so many arrows pointing to Uganda, having a real live person reach out to me seemed...different. So I took a chance and got to know Patrick.

But he was probably a scammer, right?

I know that's what you're probably thinking, because that's what I was thinking, and it's what everyone I've told part of this story to has thought. So I did some due diligence. Here's what I found:

- I found the website for the school independently and reached out to Patrick's mentor, Segawa Ephraim, via the website's email prior to Patrick mentioning him.

- Mr. Segawa responded via the email I found on the website verifying Patrick's story and his relationship to the school.

- Mr. Segawa happened to be on a visit to New Jersey about the time I was in New York; he was visiting some organizations that had sponsored his work in the past.

- I followed up with the people and organizations from the U.S. who have supported Nansana in the past. I had a long conversation with one person, Vincent, who works with the UN, and who visited the orphanage and school Mr. Segawa runs. Vincent was so moved by what he saw that he worked to raise more than $15,000 to purchase agricultural land for Mr. Segawa and his team grow food for the kids. He has also written about Patrick and his work, drawing on his firsthand experience as a visitor.

● I had another conversation with a young man named Aaron from upstate New York who volunteered at the school ten years ago and has been back several times since. He traveled from his current home in D.C. to visit Mr. Segawa when he was in the U.S., and he attested to the remarkable work Mr. Segawa has done.

● I connected with another person who happens to live near me, who has also visited the orphanage and schools and can vouch for Patrick and the project.

So to sum up, Patrick really did work at the school, and the school is really what he presented it to be.

So why do I, and maybe you, still feel uneasy about knowing they need our help? I can't answer that question for you, but here's my answer.

In the U.S., there's a comfortable structure for helping people who need help. You give money to an organization, and the organization vets people's needs and provides you evidence that your gift mattered.

But in a place like Uganda, where poverty and need are high, government corruption is rampant, and social institutions are less stable, things aren't always as easy.

So what do you do?

A few years ago, I developed a personal mission statement, and I started using it as a reference point for how I spend my time and money. It's three simple priorities:

Love God
Love the People God Gives Me
Use What God Gives Me for Him

Each day I write out these headings on a piece of paper and list what in my day will fall into these buckets. It shapes many of my decisions. And that second bucket, "the people God gives me," is a blessedly full one with concentric circles of the people you would normally think of – family, work, friends, community. There are also some regular in-breakers – people I bump into on the street, for instance, or the other people on Facebook who send me friend requests – that God also gives me, but stay in an outer circle of my attention. Over a span of days, as I wrote out those three headings, it became harder and harder to say that those are my mission goals, if I chose to ignore someone who, through a rapid confluence of reference points, God seems to have intentionally given me.

Still, Patrick couldn't be much more different from me. Difference is scary; it's written into our nature. At the time I met Patrick, though, I had recognized that our culture over-programs us toward fear, and had started an organization called Love Not Fear, which tried to raise awareness of the way media shapes us to be fearful, and to guide people to shape their media and their time to better be able to choose love instead of fear, especially when encountering someone who is different. How could I champion Love Not Fear while choosing fear when faced with someone who needs love?

• • • •

When it grew late, his disciples came to him and said, "This is a deserted place, and the hour is now very late; send them away so that they may go into the surrounding country and villages and buy something for themselves to eat." But he answered them, "You give them something to eat." They said to him, "Are we to go and buy two hundred denarii worth of bread, and give it to them to eat?" And he said to them, "How many loaves have you? Go and see." When they had found out, they said, "Five, and two fish." Then he ordered them to get all the people to sit down in groups on the green grass. So they sat down in groups of hundreds and of fifties. Taking the five loaves and the two fish, he looked up to heaven, and blessed and broke the loaves, and gave them to his disciples to set before the people; and he divided the two fish among them all. And all ate and were filled; and they took up twelve baskets full of broken pieces and of the fish. Those who had eaten the loaves numbered five thousand men. – Mark 6:35-44

"This has sh*t show potential" is not a phrase I can find coming from the disciples in any translation I've seen, but it wouldn't be hard to imagine one of them muttering the Aramaic equivalent as he (let's face it, probably Thomas) assessed the situation. Five thousand men, plus women and children. Five loaves of bread and two fish. Yeah, that could go poorly.

• • • •

After I first wrote about my friend Patrick in Uganda and the unlikely story of our connection, there were some ebbs and flows in the effort to sustain the school. We raised enough money for a water filter... but Facebook's Network for Good was slow to get the money to the U.S.-based nonprofit that supports the school. Patrick was able to raise some money for desks for the kids, but the school year was briefly thrown into chaos by a teacher strike, which reshuffled their fundraising priorities. He was able to raise money to buy supplies for their agricultural venture, but they added scores of new students from South Sudan who had fled their country to a refugee settlement and saw this hanging-by-a-thread school as a better chance to a better life. Even though they didn't have enough for the kids already under their roof, they couldn't turn away these others in even more dire need. So it was up and down. Throughout, Patrick and I messaged each other most days.

Then one day, Patrick reached out to ask if we could send clothes to the kids. As they began a new school year there, some of the new arrivals didn't have clothes, especially shoes. Could I send some from the U.S.? I explained to Patrick that, if I had the money to ship clothes from America to Uganda, it would be better for all involved just to send the money directly to the school so they could buy their own clothes. But I didn't have that kind of money.

Oh. Hey, Mr. Segawa (the school's founder, Segawa Ephraim) is planning to visit the U.S., but I think he's too far for you to see him. He's going to a conference in Hartford, Connecticut. (Yes, it's too far.)

Patrick, if we could get some clothes to Mr. Segawa could he take them back?

He could take two suitcases full – up to 23 kg (50 pounds) each.

Thus began what one of the semi-willing co-conspirators confessed had sh*t show potential.

· · · ·

I started off thinking that we could collect clothes in Florida and ship them to Hartford, but the first wake-up call was that Mr. Segawa was leaving for the U.S. that day, and would be returning less than a week later. That pretty quickly scrapped the idea of collecting and shipping. Not enough time to marshal the troops, and too expensive to ship on that time frame.

I know, basically, one person in Hartford, Connecticut, so I asked her if she knew anyone who might be able to donate clothes for kids 5 to 15 to a guy who would take them back to Uganda to orphans and refugees. (Confession: every time I tried to explain this project to someone, I ended up laughing at how absurdly unlikely it is.) I figured, best case, she'd know of a nonprofit in town I could pitch. Instead, she turned to her friends, several of whom, apparently, have *lots* of kids' clothes they don't need. In the span of about a day, it looked like our biggest concern would be that we had more than two suitcases full for Segawa to take back. All we needed to do was get the clothes to the Super 8 Hartford where he would be staying the night before he returned home, and we'd actually make this happen! My friend is a superstar who went above and beyond, and her friends were awesome to respond so quickly and abundantly.

Then we realized he didn't actually have suitcases. (This would be when the sh*t show potential comment came.) I assured my friend that, yes, this was pretty chaotic, but I was confident we could get suitcases. She didn't seem convinced, but she said she'd keep working on clothes and look to me to work my magic on suitcases.

It turned out I didn't need to. Before I heard back from a friend who is a Franciscan priest in St. Pete, who used to be a pastor in Hartford, and who said there were plenty of old suitcases that friars had left behind in the friary there, my friend's friends had scared up two suitcases to carry the shoes and clothes back with Mr. Segawa.

Through it all, I kept in steady communication with Mr. Amish, the manager of the Super 8. He was less than enthused, but handled the chaos relatively well – packages, suitcases, bags of clothes coming in at odd times for a guest who wasn't arriving for a couple days. By the last drop off, he was ready for Segawa to arrive so he could hand over all this stuff. But at the end of the day, he did his part. Sunday night I got word from Mr. Segawa that Mr. Amish had given him the suitcases, bags and packages.

· · · ·

There is a modern reinterpretation of the feeding of the multitudes, the miracle of the loaves and fishes, which is assuredly not what the gospel writers had in mind. In it, it's not so much that Jesus says "Shazam" over the bowls of breadcrumbs and multiplies them. It's that, by encouraging the one small soul who gave what he had, and tearing it into small pieces, he convinced everyone in the crowd that if they all took what they had squirreled away *just in case* and threw it in with the others, there would be enough for everyone. There is something terribly daunting about taking on the responsibility of feeding 5,000+. There is something imminently doable about throwing in the crumbs you have on you to contribute to the good of the group. It still takes some goodness and some trust, but you can do it. And when 5,000 do it, there is more than enough for everyone.

That is the sort of miracle that happened at the Super 8 Hartford that weekend. A total stranger from the other side of the world needed clothes for the kids back home who had nothing. Friends of friends of friends of his heard about it and looked for what they and their friends could spare. And he went home with two suitcases, full to the brim with hope and clothes and shoes of all kinds.

Let those with ears to hear, listen up.

• • • •

All of this happened before the COVID pandemic of 2020. You may recall how incredibly difficult that time was here. Imagine what it was like for an orphanage on the outskirts of Kampala, Uganda.

As the number of kids needing help continued to outpace the resources of the school, Patrick made a decision to replicate the experience he had at Mr. Segawa's school by starting his own effort. He raised money to purchase land that he farms so that he can provide food for the more than 150 children under his care. His organization, the Light the Future Foundation, continues to grow with the help of individual donors and an American 501c3 that some friends started called Ignite the Future, Inc. I haven't stayed in as close contact with Patrick during this time, but I continue to support Ignite the Future and both they and Patrick keep me updated on all the needs they have.

I'm telling you all this because I wanted you to know where any profits from this book are going. Look, this is my first book, and I plan to badger all of my friends until they not only buy a copy for themselves but purchase it for anyone they think would read it. I am writing this book because I want people to read it.

But the thing is, I have a day job that provides what I need at this point, so I feel a little icky pushing people to buy a book that could in theory generate profits for me that I don't need. I can push it a lot harder if it's not lining my pocket with money. (Someday, if I go pro at this in retirement, I will have a different mindset about this, I promise you.) So I decided that I want to donate any profits from this endeavor to someone who really could use the money, and I don't know anyone who needs it more than the kids Patrick is working for.

So please buy copies for all your friends and family! You can also donate directly to Ignite The Future at https://ignitethefuture.blog/

Books:

Boyle, Gregory, S.J.

Tattoos on the Heart. Free Press, 2010.
Barking at the Choir. Simon & Schuster, 2017.
Forgive Everyone Everything. Loyola Press, 2022.
The Whole Language. Avid Reader Press, 2021.

Goff, Bob. *Everybody, Always.* Thomas Nelson, 2018.

Jacobs, Bert and John. *Life is Good: The Book.* National Geographic, 2015.

Merton, Thomas. *Conjectures of a Guilty Bystander.* Image Books, 1968.

Rolheiser, Ronald, O.M.I..

The Holy Longing. Crown Publishing Group, 1999.
Our One Great Act of Fidelity. Image, 2015.

Thibodeaux, Mark. *Ascending with Ignatius: A 30-Day At-Home Retreat.* Loyola Press, 2021.

Pope Francis. "Laudato Si'." Vatican Website, 24 May 2015.

· · · ·

TV and Movies:

Ted Lasso. Created by Bill Lawrence, Jason Sudeikis, Joe Kelly, and Brendan Hunt, Apple TV+, 2020-2023.

The Family Man. Directed by Brett Ratner, Universal Pictures, 2000.

The Mission. Directed by Roland Joffé, Warner Bros., 1986.

Wall Street. Directed by Oliver Stone, 20th Century Fox, 1987.

. . . .

<u>Other Media:</u>

"Imagine." America Media, 2020. Podcast.

McDermott, Jim. "Pop Culture Spirit Wow, Episode 823." Substack, 24 July 2023, jimmcdermott.substack.com.

"Postmodern Jukebox." YouTube, www.youtube.com/@postmodernjukebox[1]

"Sundays with Ascension." YouTube,www.youtube.com/@SundayswithAscension[2].

---

1.   http://www.youtube.com/@postmodernjukebox

2.   http://www.youtube.com/@SundayswithAscension

Acknowledgements

I am grateful to so many people for the roles they played in this book. It was never my desire to write a book or become an author; I can't name all the people whose urging has led to this. This writing and publishing journey has introduced me to so many wonderful people who have given me just enough of a nudge to keep me going. But I have to thank a few people who played essential roles in this becoming a reality.

To April, my wife, best friend and partner in all things, for your unwavering support for this and all my other unlikely ideas.

To Betsy, the only reader of my first book and first reader of this one. In many ways this book is for you.

To my first non-familial readers, Tony Copeland and Amy Mangan. Thanks for your validation that this is the book you were asking for.

To Jan Boutte, for being such a phenomenal friend, editor and pep talk-giver.

To Tamara Lush, for sage advice that showed me a path when all I saw were roadblocks.

To Dave Bruns, for reigniting his "Jeff whisperer" powers and for paving the way with Ignite the Future.

To Nancy, Kristin and Joan, and Beth, Gary and Dave, for your unflagging cheerleading.

To Carin and the patient designers at GetCovers and the good folks at Draft2Digital.

To all the encouragers who offered their connections, networks, prayers, ideas, or just good thoughts for me on this journey. This book only exists because you asked for it. Thanks especially for the A Team for spreading the word.

Of course, most of all, thanks to God, for a million reasons, none more than this: on my own, I'm a horrible writer with nothing to say.

Anything worth reading here has come from me asking God what I should say.

About the Author

Jeff Johnson is a self-described "undercover theologian" whose unique journey bridges the worlds of faith, public policy, and social impact. With a Master of Divinity from Emory University's Candler School of Theology, Johnson's path took an unexpected turn from doctoral studies in Christian political thought, through a detour into sports marketing and media relations, to a distinguished career in nonprofit advocacy.

Since 2010, Johnson has led advocacy and community engagement efforts for a major nonpartisan, nonprofit advocacy organization in Florida and held volunteer leadership positions on the boards of several statewide organizations. Johnson's influence has earned him recognition as a "Florida Icon" by *Florida Trend* magazine and consistent inclusion in media lists of Florida's most influential leaders.

Despite his secular success, Johnson's theological passion persists. Since 2013, inspired by Pope Francis, Johnson has shared theological reflections on his blog, ReadingFrancis.com, and with his Facebook community, exploring the intersection of faith, culture, and everyday life.

Abandoning Temples is Johnson's first book, drawing from years of spiritual insights and diverse professional experiences to examine modern idolatry and authentic faith. His writing has also appeared in *America Magazine*, where he connected pop culture with papal teachings on aging.

Johnson lives in St. Petersburg, Florida, with his wife and daughter, continuing to bridge the gap between spiritual reflection and practical impact in both his professional and personal life. Connect with him at AbandoningTemples@gmail.com

Read more at ReadingFrancis.com.

www.ingramcontent.com/pod-product-compliance
Lightning Source LLC
Chambersburg PA
CBHW051514150726
47997CB00001B/246